Contents

Contents

Name ______________________________

Strategy Workshop

As you listen to the story "A Mummy Mystery," by Andrew Clements, you will stop from time to time to do some activities on these practice pages. These activities will help you think about different strategies that can help you read better. After completing each activity, you will discuss what you've written with your classmates and talk about how to use these strategies.

Remember, strategies can help you become a better reader. Good readers

- use strategies whenever they read
- use different strategies before, during, and after reading
- think about how strategies will help them

Name ______________________

Strategy 1: Predict/Infer

Use this strategy before and during reading to help make predictions about what happens next or what you're going to learn.

Here's how to use the Predict/Infer Strategy:

1. Think about the title, the illustrations, and what you have read so far.
2. Tell what you think will happen next—or what you will learn.
3. Thinking about what you already know on the topic may help.
4. Try to figure out things the author does not say directly.

Listen as your teacher begins "A Mummy Mystery." When your teacher stops, complete the activity to show that you understand how to predict what the story might be about and what the mystery might be.

Think about the story and respond to the question below.

What do you think the story is about, and what might the mystery be?

____

____

____

____

____

As you continue listening to the story, think about whether your prediction was right. You might want to change your prediction or write a new one below.

____

____

____

____

____

Name ______________________________

Strategy 2: Phonics/Decoding

Use this strategy during reading when you come across a word you don't know.

Here's how to use the Phonics/Decoding Strategy:

1. Look carefully at the word.
2. Look for word parts you know and think about the sounds for the letters.
3. Blend the sounds to read the words.
4. Ask yourself: is this a word I know? Does it make sense in what I am reading?
5. If not, ask yourself what else can I try? Should I look in a dictionary?

Listen as your teacher continues the story. When your teacher stops, use the Phonics/Decoding Strategy.

Now write down the steps you used to decode the word *Dynasty*.

____

____

____

____

____

____

____

____

____

____

____

Remember to use this strategy whenever you are reading and come across a word that you don't know.

Name ______________________________

Strategy 3: Monitor/Clarify

Use this strategy during reading whenever you're confused about what you are reading.

Here's how to use the Monitor/Clarify Strategy:

- Ask yourself if what you're reading makes sense—or if you are learning what you need to learn.
- If you don't understand something, reread, use the illustrations, or read ahead to see if that helps.

Listen as your teacher continues the story. When your teacher stops, complete the activity to show that you understand what's happening in the story.

Think about the mummy and respond below.

1. Describe what happened with the mummy's hand.

____

____

____

____

2. Can you tell from listening to the story how everyone reacts to the mummy's hand moving? Why or why not?

____

____

____

____

3. How can you find out what made the mummy's hand move?

____

____

____

____

Name ________________________________

Strategy 4: Question

Use this strategy during and after reading to ask questions about important ideas in the story.

Here's how to use the Question Strategy:

- Ask yourself questions about important ideas in the story.
- Ask yourself if you can answer these questions.
- If you can't answer the questions, reread and look for answers in the text. Thinking about what you already know and what you've read in the story may help you.

Listen as your teacher continues the story. Then complete the activity to show that you understand how to ask yourself questions about important ideas in the story.

Think about the story and respond below.

Write a question you might ask yourself at this point in the story.

____

____

____

____

____

____

____

If you can't answer your question now, think about it while you listen to the rest of the story.

Name ______________________

Strategy 5: Evaluate

Use this strategy during and after reading to help you form an opinion about what you read.

Here's how to use the Evaluate Strategy:

- Tell whether or not you think this story is entertaining and why.
- Is the writing clear and easy to understand?
- This is a mystery story. Did the author make the characters believable and interesting?

Listen as your teacher continues the story. When your teacher stops, complete the activity to show that you are thinking of how you feel about what you are reading and why you feel that way.

Think about the story and respond below.

1. Tell whether or not you think this story is entertaining and why.

____

____

____

____

2. Is the writing clear and easy to understand?

____

____

____

____

3. This is a mystery story. Did the author make the characters interesting and believable?

____

____

____

____

Name ______________________________

Strategy 6: Summarize

Use this strategy after reading to summarize what you read.

Here's how to use the Summarize Strategy:

- Think about the characters.
- Think about where the story takes place.
- Think about the problem in the story and how the characters solve it.
- Think about what happens in the beginning, middle, and end of the story.

Think about the story you just listened to. Complete the activity to show that you understand how to identify important story parts that will help you summarize the story.

Think about the story and respond to the questions below:

1. Who is the main character?

____

____

____

2. Where does the story take place?

____

____

____

____

3. What is the problem and how is it resolved?

____

____

____

____

Now use this information to summarize the story for a partner.

Name ______________________________

Courage

The characters in this theme show courage in dangerous or challenging situations. After reading each selection, complete the chart below to show what you learned about the characters.

	Hatchet	Passage to Freedom
What challenge does the main character face?		
Where does the challenge take place?		
In what ways does the main character show courage?		
What do you think the character learns from his or her experience?		

Name ____________________

Courage continued

	Climb or Die	The True Confessions of Charlotte Doyle
What challenge does the main character face?		
Where does the challenge take place?		
In what ways does the main character show courage?		
What do you think the character learns from his or her experience?		

What have you learned about courage in this theme?

____

____

Name ______________________________

Words in the Wild

Answer each of the following questions by writing a vocabulary word.

Vocabulary

- hatchet
- quills
- shelter
- survival
- terrified
- frustration
- slithering
- kindling

1. Which word tells what you should seek in a rainstorm so you won't get wet? ____________________
2. Which word describes what a snake is doing when it moves across the ground? ____________________
3. Which word names a tool used to chop wood? ____________________
4. Which word describes small pieces of wood needed to build a fire? ____________________
5. Which word means "very frightened"? ____________________
6. Which word names the sharp spines a porcupine uses to defend itself? ____________________
7. Which word means "the process of staying alive"? ____________________
8. Which word describes a feeling a person has when he or she keeps trying to do something but cannot do it? ____________________

Write two questions of your own that use vocabulary words from the list above.

9. ____
10. ____

Name ______________________________

Details Chart

Page(s)	Brian feels _____.	Details that show how Brian feels
30	terrified	
32–33		• the eight quills in his leg seem like dozens • his pain spreads • catches his breath when he pulls the quills out
33–34		• He thinks, "I can't take this" and "I can't do this." • He cries until he is cried out.
34–35	frustrated	
36–37		• realizes the hatchet can make sparks • recognizes the message about fire from his dreams • begins to make sparks to start a fire
38–41	determined	
43	satisfied	

Name ______________________________

What Really Happened?

These sentences tell about Brian and the things that happen to him in the story. Write T if the sentence is true. Write F if the sentence is false. If the sentence is false, correct it to make it true.

1. _____ Brian wakes up when he hears a bear growling outside his shelter.

____

2. _____ Brian's leg gets injured when he kicks out in the darkness and hits the hatchet.

____

3. _____ After crying for a long time, Brian realizes that feeling sorry for yourself changes nothing.

____

4. _____ Seeing his father and his friend Terry in a dream makes Brian feel happy.

____

5. _____ In Brian's dream, his friend Terry shows him a path out of the forest.

____

6. _____ Brian thinks that throwing his hatchet to protect himself from wild animals is a bad idea.

____

7. _____ By hitting the hatchet against a hard black rock, Brian is able to make sparks.

____

Name ______________________________

Seeing the Solution

Read the story. Then complete the activity on page 15.

The Water Tree

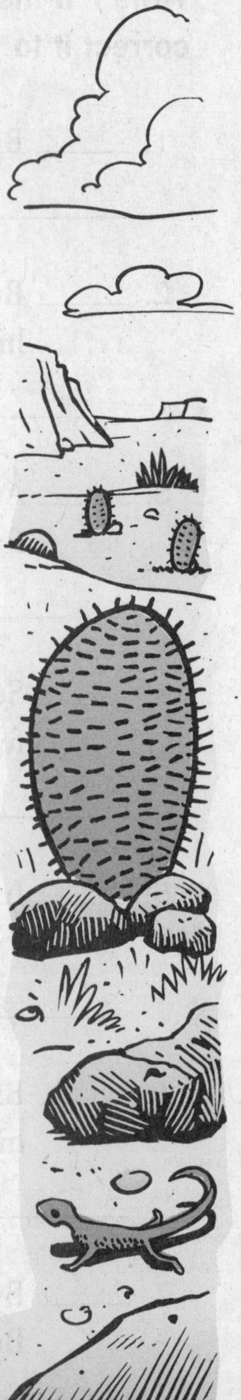

Paul and I had been hiking for six hours. We came upon a dry creekbed that ran through the desert. Paul frowned, and I sighed. "I hope this isn't the creek we've been trying to reach," I said.

"See, Tom, I told you we should have brought more water," said Paul. Between the two of us, we had only about a third of a bottle left. Our clothes were wet with sweat and our throats were dry, but we dared not drink any more water yet. Even if we headed back right away, it was at least a six-hour hike back to our campground.

Paul and I just stared at the dry creekbed. "Check the map," I said to Paul. "Is there any other water within a mile of here?" I thought that even if there was another creek nearby, it might be dry too.

"There's nothing but lava rocks and an occasional cactus for another three miles," he reported grimly as he pulled out his map. Then his eyes lit up. "Wait a second, Tom," he said in a much happier voice. "A cactus!" He grinned and slapped me on the back.

"A cactus what?" I said. I wondered how he could be so excited about desert plants at a time like this.

"Don't you remember what we learned at camp last summer?" Paul asked. Then my own face curled into a smile. At camp they had shown us how to get water from a cactus.

"Do you have a knife?" I asked. "I have a handkerchief we can use to strain the water from the cactus flesh." Within minutes we were squeezing water out of a prickly pear cactus into our water bottles, through a funnel fashioned from a sun visor. We didn't get much water per squeeze, but there were more than enough cacti around. We'd make it back to camp with water to spare.

Name ______________________________

Seeing the Solution continued

Answer these questions about the story on page 14.

1. How do Paul and Tom feel when they reach the dry creekbed? Why?

____

____

2. What details in the first paragraph help you figure out how the boys feel?

____

3. What kind of danger are the boys in? What details help you understand the danger?

____

____

____

4. How does Paul feel when he remembers that they can get water from a cactus? How do you know his feelings change?

____

____

5. How do the boys make use of what they have to get water?

____

____

6. Do you think that the task of filling the water bottles will be a fast one or a slow one? Why?

____

____

Name ______________________________

Suffixes Aflame

Circle the words with the suffixes *-ful, -less,* and *-ly* in the flames.
Use the circled words to complete the story.

Brian's strange dream at first seemed ______________________, until he realized that he needed a fire. In one ______________________ after another, he gathered tiny bits of ______________________ white birch bark. He made a nest out of the ______________________ fine bits of bark, but it stayed alight only ______________________. He seemed ______________________ to keep the flame going. ______________________, he discovered how to fan the flames with his breath. In time, he would become ______________________ at building a fire.

Which word has *two* suffixes?

____

Name ______________________________

Short Vowels

A short vowel sound is usually spelled *a, e, i, o,* or *u* and is followed by a consonant sound.

/ă/ cr**a**ft   /ĕ/ d**e**pth   /ĭ/ f**i**lm   /ŏ/ b**o**mb   /ŭ/ pl**u**nge

Write each Spelling Word under its short vowel sound.

/ă/ Sound

________________ ________________

/ĕ/ Sound

________________ ________________

________________ ________________

____

/ĭ/ Sound

________________ ________________

________________ ________________

________________ ________________

/ŏ/ Sound

________________ ________________

/ŭ/ Sound

________________ ________________

________________ ________________

____

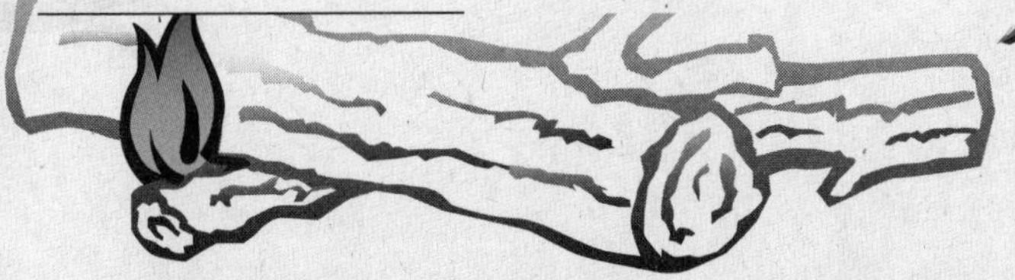

Spelling Words

1. depth
2. craft
3. plunge
4. wreck
5. sunk
6. film
7. wince
8. bomb
9. switch
10. length
11. prompt
12. pitch
13. else
14. cliff
15. pledge
16. scrub
17. brass
18. grill
19. stung
20. bulk

Name ____________________________

Spelling Spree

Change the Word **Write a Spelling Word by adding one letter to each word below.**

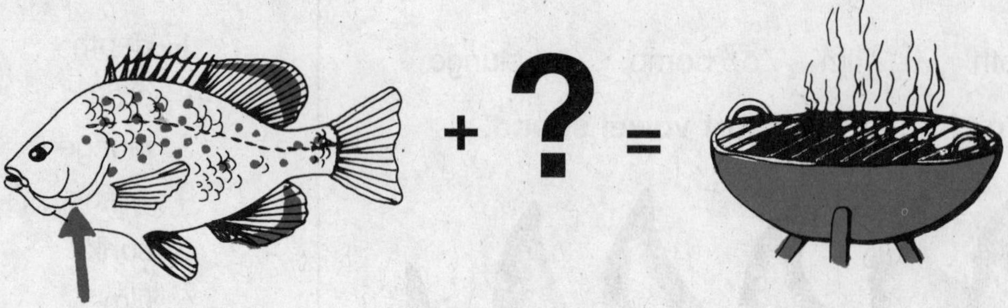

1. ledge ____________
2. bass ____________
3. sun ____________
4. itch ____________
5. raft ____________
6. wine ____________
7. lunge ____________
8. gill ____________
9. bob ____________
10. sung ____________

Word Detective **Write a Spelling Word to fit each clue.**

11. great size or volume ____________
12. the measure of being long ____________
13. something used in a camera ____________
14. an overhanging rock face ____________
15. other or different ____________
16. what's left after a crash ____________
17. the quality of being deep ____________
18. a device used to turn on the power ____________
19. to clean very well ____________
20. right on time ____________

Spelling Words

1. depth
2. craft
3. plunge
4. wreck
5. sunk
6. film
7. wince
8. bomb
9. switch
10. length
11. prompt
12. pitch
13. else
14. cliff
15. pledge
16. scrub
17. brass
18. grill
19. stung
20. bulk

Name ______________________________

Proofreading and Writing

Proofreading Circle the five misspelled Spelling Words in this journal entry. Then write each word correctly.

I spent all day today starting a fire. Building a fire is a real craft! I began by trying to light pieces of a torn twenty-dollar bill. Then I decided to swich to strips of birch bark. I gathered some pieces of the right lenth and width and made them into a ball. I lit the ball with the sparks made by striking my hatchet against the rock wall. It was hard work, but I don't know what els I could have used to start the fire. I still winse when I think about another night without one. My next goal is to figure out how to make a gril that I can cook on.

1. ____________________
2. ____________________
3. ____________________
4. ____________________
5. ____________________

Spelling Words

1. depth
2. craft
3. plunge
4. wreck
5. sunk
6. film
7. wince
8. bomb
9. switch
10. length
11. prompt
12. pitch
13. else
14. cliff
15. pledge
16. scrub
17. brass
18. grill
19. stung
20. bulk

Write an Opinion What do you think about the way the writer of this journal entry went about building a fire? Was there anything about his or her behavior that you admired? Is there anything you would have done differently?

On a separate piece of paper, write a paragraph in which you give your opinion of the writer's way of doing things. Use Spelling Words from the list.

Name ______________________________

A Search for Meaning

Your friend doesn't know the meaning of some words in a story she's reading. Use context clues to help her figure out the underlined words, and then fill in the chart.

From a safe distance, Marcy squatted low and watched the burning storage barn. The flames were consuming one section after another, as though the building were an enormous meal. The fire left almost nothing behind, so she thought all the building materials must be flammable. She was gratified to hear sirens in the distance. Her 911 call had been heard.

Word	Clues from Context	Meaning
squatted		
consuming		
flammable		
gratified		

Name ___________________________

What Is a Spiny Pig?

Kinds of Sentences A **declarative** sentence makes a statement. It ends with a **period**. An **interrogative** sentence asks a question. It ends with a **question mark**. An **imperative** sentence gives an order or makes a request. It ends with a **period**. An **exclamatory** sentence shows excitement or strong feeling. It ends with an **exclamation point**.

Add the correct end punctuation to each sentence. Then label each sentence *declarative, interrogative, imperative,* or *exclamatory*.

1. Porcupines are rodents ___________________
2. They have long, sharp quills ___________________
3. Treat all animals with respect ___________________
4. Have you ever seen a porcupine ___________________
5. How big the tail is ___________________
6. Do porcupines have fine or coarse fur ___________________
7. Please let me see your porcupine quill ___________________
8. What a sharp tip it has ___________________
9. Did you know the word *porcupine* means "spiny pig" in Latin ___________________
10. *Porcupine* comes from Latin *porcus* (meaning "pig") and *spina* (meaning "spine") ___________________

Name ______________________________

Campfires Need . . .

Subjects and Predicates The **subject** of a sentence tells whom or what the sentence is about. The **complete subject** includes all the words in the subject. The **simple subject** is the main word or words of the complete subject.

The **predicate** tells what the subject does, is, has, or feels. The **complete predicate** includes all the words in the predicate. The **simple predicate** is the main word or words of the complete predicate.

Draw a line between the complete subject and the complete predicate in each sentence below. Then write the simple subject and the simple predicate on the lines.

1. Brianna needed kindling for a fire.

   Simple subject: ______________________

   Simple predicate: ______________________

2. A fire needs oxygen.

   Simple subject: ______________________

   Simple predicate: ______________________

3. A roaring fire will keep them warm.

   Simple subject: ______________________

   Simple predicate: ______________________

4. The first spark has faded quickly.

   Simple subject: ______________________

   Simple predicate: ______________________

5. I am learning about building safe campfires.

   Simple subject: ______________________

   Simple predicate: ______________________

Name ______________________

This and That

Combining Sentences A good writer avoids writing too many short, choppy sentences. Combine short sentences by creating **compound subjects** or **compound predicates.**

Moose live in these woods.
Caribou live in these woods too.

Compound Subject
Moose and caribou live in these woods.

I ate quickly.
I gulped my juice.

Compound Predicate
I ate quickly and gulped my juice.

Combine subjects or predicates in each group of sentences below.

Example: I sighed. Then I sat down.
I sighed and sat down.

1. Rebecca was prepared for an emergency.
The other hikers were prepared for an emergency.

____

2. The scout built the fire.
The scout stoked the fire.

____

3. Hatchets should be used with caution.
Axes should be used with caution.
Other sharp tools should be used with caution.

____

4. The birch trees swayed in the wind.
The birch trees creaked in the wind.

____

5. Conrad will gather wood.
Sam will gather wood.

____

Name ______________________________

Writing Instructions

In *Hatchet*, Brian is stranded alone in the Canadian wilderness. The only tool he has is a hatchet. How could Brian explain to someone else how he used the hatchet to start a fire? **Instructions** tell readers how to do or make something. Good written instructions clearly explain the materials needed and the order in which the steps are to be followed.

Use this page to plan and organize your own written instructions. First, choose a process you would like to explain. Then list the materials that are needed. Finally, write each step in the process, giving details that readers will need to know.

How to ______________________________

Materials	
Steps	**Details**
Step 1	
Step 2	
Step 3	
Step 4	
Step 5	

Using the information you recorded, write your instructions on a separate sheet of paper. You can either number each step or use sequence words such as *first*, *next*, and *finally*. Include diagrams or pictures to help readers picture this process.

Name ______________________________

Using Sequence Words and Phrases

Following steps correctly is a matter of life or death for Brian in *Hatchet*. A careful writer gives clear instructions so that a reader can complete the steps in a process. Sequence words and phrases in instructions help readers understand a process and keep track of the order of steps.

The following page is from a first-aid manual. The instructions tell readers how to treat puncture wounds like those Brian suffered from the porcupine quills in his leg. In the blanks provided, add sequence words and phrases from the list to make the connection between steps clearer. Remember to capitalize sequence words as needed.

Sequence Words and Phrases

first	after	by the time
during	prior to	finally
before	then	as soon as possible

______________________, you will need to wash your hands with soap and water. ______________________ you have washed your hands, remove the object with a pair of tweezers. ______________________ control any bleeding with direct pressure and elevation. Wash the puncture wound thoroughly with soap and water. ______________________, cover the wound with a sterile dressing.

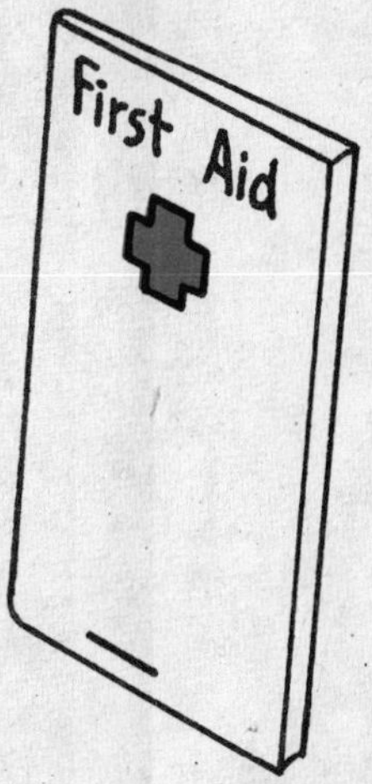

Check with a doctor to find out whether a tetanus shot is needed. If you see any signs of infection, such as pus, pain, redness around the wound, or a fever, call the doctor back ______________________.

Name ______________________________

Revising Your Personal Narrative

Reread your narrative. Put a checkmark in the box for each sentence that describes your paper. Use this page to help you revise.

Loud and Clear!

- ☐ The beginning catches the reader's interest.
- ☐ All events are focused on a single experience. They are also told in order.
- ☐ Many details and exact words bring the story to life.
- ☐ My writing sounds like me. You can tell how I feel.
- ☐ Sentences flow smoothly, and there are few mistakes.

Sounding Stronger

- ☐ The beginning could be more interesting.
- ☐ A few events are out of order, and a few are unrelated.
- ☐ More details and exact words are needed.
- ☐ My voice could be stronger. It doesn't always sound like me.
- ☐ The sentences don't always flow smoothly. There are some mistakes.

Turn Up the Volume

- ☐ The beginning is missing or weak.
- ☐ The story is not focused. The order is unclear.
- ☐ There are no details or exact words.
- ☐ I can't hear my voice at all.
- ☐ Most sentences are choppy. Mistakes make it hard to read.

Name ______________________

Improving Your Writing

Varying Sentences **Rewrite the paragraphs in the spaces provided. Each paragraph should include at least one example of each type of sentence: declarative, interrogative, imperative, and exclamatory.**

Backstage Pass NO SENTENCE VARIATION I shook hands with Whole New Crew! I was at their concert! I went backstage! I met Jeff! I met Pinky! I met Wanda! I met Therese! At first, I was so excited I could hardly breathe! And guess what — they ignored me! After a while it got boring! So we went home!	**Backstage Pass** SENTENCE VARIATION ______ ______ ______ ______ ______
Jalapeño Biscuits NO SENTENCE VARIATION Do I know how to make biscuits? Sort of. Did I put in the flour, butter, and baking powder? I did. Did I add jalapeño peppers? Accidentally. What did it taste like? It was sort of good. Then why did I end up running to get a drink of water? Because it was so HOT.	**Jalapeño Biscuits** SENTENCE VARIATION ______ ______ ______ ______ ______
Early Start NO SENTENCE VARIATION The coach said to meet at 6 A.M. for Saturday's game. Anyone late would not play, the coach said. On Friday, I set my alarm for 5. I went to the field. Everyone was there — except the coach. We finally found her. Her car had broken down. She said, "I guess I don't get to play."	**Early Start** SENTENCE VARIATION ______ ______ ______ ______ ______

Name ______________________________

Spelling Words

Most of the Spelling Words on this list are often misspelled because they are **homophones,** words that sound alike but have different meanings and spellings. Look for familiar spelling patterns to help you remember how to spell the words on this page. Think carefully about the parts that you find hard to spell in each word.

Write the missing letters and apostrophes in the Spelling Words below.

1. y ____ ____ ____
2. you ____ ____ ____
3. th ____ ____ r
4. th ____ r ____
5. th ____ ____ ____ re
6. it ____
7. it ____ ____
8. w ____ ____ ____ dn't
9. we ____ ____ ____
10. t ____
11. t ____ ____
12. tha ____ ____ ____
13. k ____ ew
14. ____ ____ ow

Spelling Words

1. your
2. you're
3. their
4. there
5. they're
6. its
7. it's
8. wouldn't
9. we're
10. to
11. too
12. that's
13. knew
14. know

Study List On a separate piece of paper, write each Spelling Word. Check your spelling against the words on the list.

Name ______________________________

Spelling Spree

Homophone Blanks **The blanks in each of the following sentences can be filled with homophones from the Spelling Word list. Write the words in the correct order.**

1–3. I think that _____ sitting over _____ on _____ blanket.
4–5. If you don't hurry, _____ going to miss _____ bus.
6–7. The pizza's still _____ hot _____ eat.
8–9. Since _____ so hot today, the school is letting _____ students go home early.

1–3. ______________________________
4–5. ______________________________
6–7. ______________________________
8–9. ______________________________

Word Addition **Write a Spelling Word by adding the beginning of the first word to the end of the second word.**

10. than + Pat's
11. we'll + score
12. knack + flew
13. work + shouldn't
14. knight + grow

10. ______________
11. ______________
12. ______________
13. ______________
14. ______________

Spelling Words

1. your
2. you're
3. their
4. there
5. they're
6. its
7. it's
8. wouldn't
9. we're
10. to
11. too
12. that's
13. knew
14. know

Name ______________________________

Proofreading and Writing

Proofreading **Circle the five misspelled Spelling Words in this poster. Then write each word correctly.**

What Is Courage?

Maybe it's sticking to you're beliefs, no matter what. Courage can also mean pushing yourself at times when most people woudn't. And if you put yourself in danger to help someone, thats courage by any definition. But even if we don't now exactly how to define it, we recognize it when we see it. And wer'e all grateful every time we do.

Spelling Words

1. your
2. you're
3. their
4. there
5. they're
6. its
7. it's
8. wouldn't
9. we're
10. to
11. too
12. that's
13. knew
14. know

1. ____________________
2. ____________________
3. ____________________
4. ____________________
5. ____________________

Writing Headlines Suppose that a newspaper were going to write articles covering the events that take place in each of the selections in this theme. What would some good headlines be?

On a separate piece of paper, write a headline for each selection in the theme. Use Spelling Words from the list.

Name ____________________

The Official Word

Read the word in each box below from *Passage to Freedom*. Then write a word from the list that is related in meaning. Use a dictionary if necessary.

Vocabulary

- bosses
- documents
- envoy
- organization
- choice
- approval
- victims

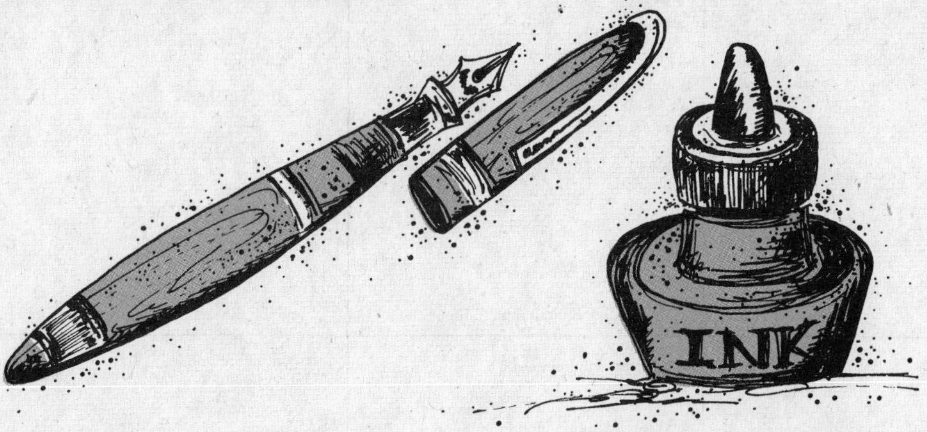

superiors	government	visas
____________	____________	____________
refugees	**diplomat**	**decision**
____________	____________	____________
	permission	
	____________	

Choose *three* words from the list above. Write a short paragraph about what Hiroki Sugihara's father did in *Passage to Freedom*.

____

____

____

____

____

Name ___________________________________

Judgments Chart

	Facts from the Selection	Own Values and Experiences	Judgment
What kind of person is Mr. Sugihara?			
Is Mr. Sugihara's decision right or wrong?			
What kind of a person is Hiroki's mother?			

Name ______________________________

Award for a Hero

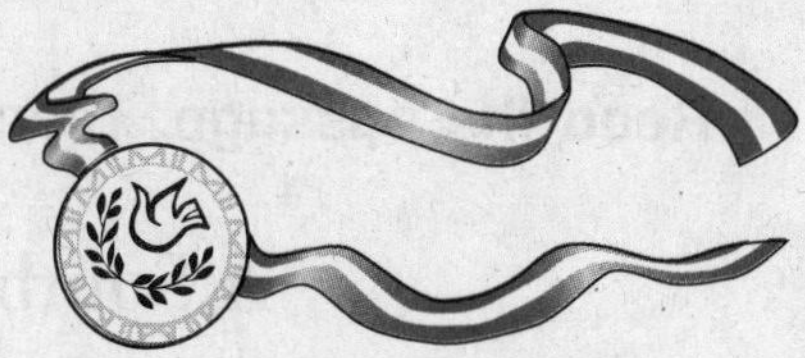

Complete the fact sheet below about Chiune Sugihara. Then on a separate sheet of paper design an award that honors Mr. Sugihara.

FACT SHEET

Who Chiune Sugihara was:	
Where he was from:	
Where he was working at the beginning of World War II:	
What his job was:	
Why people needed his help:	
What conflict he faced:	
What decision he made:	
Why he is remembered:	

Name ______________________________

Judge for Yourself

Read the passage. Then answer the questions on page 35.

A South African Hero

In 1918, Nelson Mandela was born into a royal African family in South Africa. He was raised to be a chief, but instead chose to become a lawyer. He hoped to help blacks win equal rights in South Africa. At the time, the country was ruled by a white minority that discriminated against blacks. This policy was later called *apartheid*.

In the 1940s, Mandela earned his law degree. He helped set up the first black law firm in South Africa. He also joined the African National Congress (ANC), a group that worked to end apartheid. Mandela soon became a top official in the ANC and a leader of nonviolent protests.

The government cracked down on the ANC, however, and responded to peaceful protests with violence. In 1960, Mandela decided to abandon nonviolence and support armed struggle against apartheid. "The government left us no other choice," he said. Arrested several times for his work, he was tried for treason in 1963. At his trial, Mandela declared, "I have cherished the ideal of a democratic and free society. . . . It is an ideal which I hope to live for and to achieve. But if needs be, it is an ideal for which I am prepared to die."

Mandela was sentenced to life in prison and spent the next twenty-seven years behind bars. The struggle for equal rights in South Africa continued, however, and people around the world called for an end to apartheid. The government offered to free Mandela in exchange for his cooperation, but he refused. Finally, in 1990, the government released him from prison. He later won the Nobel Peace Prize and became South Africa's first black president. As president, Mandela called for peace and harmony in South Africa and tried to ensure equal rights for all South Africans.

Name ______________________________

Judge for Yourself continued

Answer these questions about the passage on page 34.

1. What was important to Nelson Mandela as a young man?

____

____

2. What facts from the passage reveal his values as a young man?

____

____

3. Circle three words you would use to describe Nelson Mandela.

selfless	compassionate	uninspired
powerless	alienated	determined

4. Write each word you circled below. Then tell why you made that judgment about Mandela's character. Use facts from the passage to support your judgment.

Word	Reasons for Judgment

5. How have your own experiences and beliefs helped you make a judgment about Nelson Mandela's character and actions?

____

____

Name ______________________________

Sugihara Syllables

Write each underlined word on the line below. Add slashes between the syllables of each word. Then write another sentence using the word correctly.

1. My father was a Japanese diplomat working in Lithuania.

____
____
____

2. Hundreds of refugees gathered outside our house.

____
____
____

3. They needed visas to leave the country.

____
____
____

4. My father replied that he would help each one of the refugees.

____
____
____

5. My life changed forever because of my father's action.

____
____
____

Name ____________________

Long Vowels

A long vowel sound may be spelled vowel-consonant-*e* or with two vowels written together.

/ā/ **ga**z**e**, tr**ai**t /ē/ th**e**m**e**, pr**ea**ch, sl**ee**ve /ī/ str**i**v**e**
/ō/ qu**o**t**e**, r**oa**m /yōō/ m**u**t**e**

Write each Spelling Word under its long vowel sound.

/ā/ Sound

____
____
____
____
____
____

/ē/ Sound

____
____
____
____
____

/ī/ Sound

____

/ō/ Sound

____
____
____
____
____

/yōō/ Sound

____
____

Spelling Words

1. theme
2. quote
3. gaze
4. pace
5. preach
6. strive
7. trait
8. mute
9. sleeve
10. roam
11. strain
12. fade
13. league
14. soak
15. grease
16. throne
17. fume
18. file
19. toast
20. brake

Name ______________________

Spelling Spree

The Third Word **Write the Spelling Word that belongs with each group of words.**

1. pocket, collar, ____________
2. association, group, ____________
3. vapor, gas, ____________
4. feature, quality, ____________
5. crown, castle, ____________
6. advise, counsel, ____________
7. passage, excerpt, ____________

Code Breaker **Some Spelling Words have been written in code. Use the code below to figure out each word. Then write the words correctly.**

CODE:	J	X	B	M	S	L	T	O	W	K	E	G	C	N	I	Z	H
LETTER:	A	B	D	E	F	G	H	I	K	L	M	O	R	S	T	U	V

8. LCMJNM ____________
9. ITMEM ____________
10. SOKM ____________
11. SJBM ____________
12. XCJWM ____________
13. IGJNI ____________
14. NGJW ____________
15. CGJE ____________

Spelling Words

1. theme
2. quote
3. gaze
4. pace
5. preach
6. strive
7. trait
8. mute
9. sleeve
10. roam
11. strain
12. fade
13. league
14. soak
15. grease
16. throne
17. fume
18. file
19. toast
20. brake

Name ______________________________

Proofreading and Writing

Proofreading Circle the five misspelled Spelling Words in this screenplay. Then write each word correctly.

Mr. Sugihara enters his home. He walks to a chair and collapses into it. He sits muet for a few seconds, and then he speaks.

MR. SUGIHARA: I've been filling out visas all day at an incredible pase. I don't know how much longer I can take the strane. . . . *(His voice begins to fade as his head droops to his chest.)*

MRS. SUGIHARA: *(She looks at her husband.)* I know, but you must think of the people. You can't just leave them to roam the countryside. They need a place to go.

MR. SUGIHARA: *(He slowly lifts his head and meets his wife's gaiz.)* You're right, of course. I should striv to help as many as I can. If I don't, what will happen to them?

1. ______________
2. ______________
3. ______________
4. ______________
5. ______________

Spelling Words

1. theme
2. quote
3. gaze
4. pace
5. preach
6. strive
7. trait
8. mute
9. sleeve
10. roam
11. strain
12. fade
13. league
14. soak
15. grease
16. throne
17. fume
18. file
19. toast
20. brake

Write a Persuasive Letter You have a chance to send Mr. Sugihara a letter on behalf of the refugees. You know he is unsure of what action to take. What will you write to convince him to help them?

On a separate piece of paper, write a persuasive letter to Mr. Sugihara. Include several reasons why he should help the refugees. Use Spelling Words from the list.

Name ______________________________

Word-Order Sets

For each set of words, decide which two would be the guide words if all three words were on a dictionary page. On each "page," write the guide words in the correct order on the first line, and the other word on the line below.

office	ceiling	gown	refugees	emergency
offer	celery	government	refuse	embody
offside	celebration	gourmet	refrigerator	embraced

Name ______________________________

Safety and Freedom

Conjunctions A **conjunction** is a word that connects words or sentences. The words *and*, *but*, and *or* are conjunctions.

In each sentence below, add a conjunction. Then on the line, write *words* or *sentences* to show what the conjunction joins.

Example: The escape was risky __and__ frightening.
__words__

1. The diplomat had courage, ________ he had compassion.
____

2. He knew it was risky, ________ he helped the people.
____

3. His children could not see their friends ________ teachers.
____

4. His wife ________ family members agreed to help.
____

5. The women, men, ________ children escaped to a safer place.
____

Name ______________________________

Should We Run, or Should We Hide?

Compound Sentences A **compound sentence** is two simple sentences joined by a comma and a conjunction (*and*, *but*, or *or*).

Add a comma followed by *and*, *but*, or *or* to combine the simple sentences below into compound sentences.

Example: Our escape was dangerous. We made it safely.
Our escape was dangerous, but we made it safely.

1. World War II brought many hardships. People showed great courage.

____

____

2. Have you read any books about that war? Did you see any movies about it?

____

____

3. Bombs fell in many places. They did not fall in America.

____

____

4. My great-grandfather was in the Navy. He showed me his uniform.

____

____

5. Our town built a war memorial in the park. My class went to see it.

____

____

Name ______________________________

I Can Speak Italian, but I Can't Speak Japanese

Combining Sentences: Compound Sentences Sometimes combining short, choppy sentences into longer sentences makes your writing more interesting. Use a comma and *and*, *but*, or *or* to combine sentences.

Lee has written a letter to Aunt Lucy. Revise the letter by combining simple sentences to make compound sentences. Insert your marks on, above, and below the line, as shown in the example. The last sentence will not change.

Tomorrow I'd like to go to the zoo, or I'd like to visit Mel.

Dear Aunt Lucy,

I think I'd like to be a diplomat someday. I don't know where I'd like to live. Italy would be an interesting place to live. I might live in Japan. You taught me to speak Italian. I don't know anyone who can teach me Japanese. Maybe I could study it in school. I could study Japanese history too. My teacher visited Japan. He showed us beautiful pictures. The next time I visit, may I see your photos of Italy?

Love,

Lee

Name ______________________________

Writing a Memo

Chiune Sugihara was a diplomat in Lithuania in 1940. He probably wrote different forms of business communication, such as letters, reports, and memos. A **memo** is a brief, informal message that is sent from one person to others in the same company, group, or organization.

Imagine that you are Mr. Sugihara. Plan and organize a memo to your superiors in the Japanese government about the plight of the Jewish refugees from Poland. Follow these steps:

1. Name the person or persons to whom you are writing the memo.
2. Tell who is writing the memo.
3. Write the date.
4. Identify the subject of the memo.
5. Write the body of the memo. Begin by stating your reason for writing. Use clear, direct language and a business-like tone. Be brief but include all the important information. If you want a response, end by asking a question or by requesting that a specific action be taken.

To: ______________________________

From: ______________________________

Date: ______________________________

Subject: ______________________________

____

____

____

____

____

Copy your memo on a separate sheet of paper and exchange it with a classmate. Then, using the format above, write a response memo from the officials in the Japanese government to Chiune Sugihara in which you deny him permission to grant visas to the Polish refugees.

Name ___________________________________

Capitalizing and Punctuating Sentences

To communicate effectively, a writer must write sentences correctly. When you write, remember to begin all sentences with a capital letter and to capitalize the names of people and places. Also, remember to end sentences with a period, a question mark, or an exclamation mark.

Proofread the following memo. Look for errors in capitalizing and punctuating sentences. Use these proofreading marks to add the necessary capital letters and end punctuation.

⊙	Add a period.	^!	Add an exclamation mark.
≡	Make a capital letter.	^?	Add a question mark.

To: Mrs. Masue Okimoto, Office Manager

From: Mr. Kenji Hamano

Date: August 25, 1940

Subject: Request for Office Supplies

my assistant boris Lavhas informed me that we need to restock some office supplies will you kindly send the items listed below ^

1. two hundred visas and permission forms
2. one dozen fountain pens
3. two dozen bottles of ink

please ship these supplies to my office in lithuania immediately ^

thank you for your prompt action in this matter

Name ______________________________

Complete the Climb

Complete each sentence about mountain climbing with the correct word from the list.

Vocabulary

carabiners
pitons
foothold
desperate
improvising
belay
ice ax
overcome
functioned
fatigue

1. Metal spikes with a hole at the end through which you pass a rope are called ______________________.
2. Metal rings you use to attach rope to pitons are called ______________________.
3. To cut into the ice and support your upper body while climbing, you might use an ______________________.
4. In order to remain steady on your feet, it is important to find a secure ______________________.
5. If you and another climber are helping each other climb up the mountain while attached to the same rope, you are on ______________________.
6. Do not push yourself too hard, or you may experience extreme ______________________.
7. If you get lost and feel nearly hopeless that help will arrive, you feel ______________________.
8. If you don't have the proper equipment, you might look for other tools you have and try ______________________.
9. If you climb cautiously and with safety in mind, you will never have to face an obstacle you won't be able to ______________________.
10. Safe climbers have always ______________________ as role models for others.

Name ______________________________

Event Chart

1. **Page 75** At first Danielle hits the rock with Dad's hammer. Then she
____

2. **Page 77** The hammers work. Next, Jake and Danielle
____

3. **Page 78** Danielle gets to the top of the trench first. Then she
____

4. **Pages 80–81** Jake and Danielle are happy to be at the top. Then they realize
____

5. **Page 82** Crying, Jake and Danielle hug each other. Then Danielle pushes Jake away. Suddenly, Jake realizes that she is
____

6. **Page 84** Through the clouds, they see
____

7. **Pages 84–85** Danielle is getting weaker. When they finally knock on the weather station door,
____

8. **Page 86** Jake improvises by ______________________________ As a result, ______________________________

Name ______________________________

Interview with the Ice Climbers

Complete the interview below by writing the answers Danielle and Jake would give to tell about their experience.

Q: Jake, why did you and your sister climb Mount Remington in the first place?

A: ______________________________

____

____

Q: Danielle, how did you and your brother manage to climb without proper equipment?

A: ______________________________

____

Q: What happened when you reached the top of the trench?

A: ______________________________

____

____

Q: Jake, how did you and your sister feel at that moment?

A: ______________________________

____

Q: What happened next that raised your spirits?

A: ______________________________

____

Q: What happened when you finally got to the weather station?

A: ______________________________

____

Name ____________________

Then What Happened?

Read the passage. Then complete the activity on page 50.

A Day Hike

"I'm so glad you're okay!" Elaine's dad said as he hugged her close. "But what were you thinking, wandering off like that?"

The events of the past hour came rushing back to Elaine. She had been hiking along behind her mom and dad, enjoying the mountain scenery and warm summer day. Then she had stopped to look at some wildflowers. The flowers spread away from the path and down into a meadow. Elaine had wandered off the trail and into the meadow. While her parents had continued hiking up the trail, Elaine had lain on her stomach, peering at hundreds of pink, yellow, and blue blossoms.

A few minutes later she had heard a sound. When she looked up, she couldn't believe her eyes. Fifty yards away stood a mountain lion, staring straight at her! Elaine had frozen, her heart pounding. Should she lie still? Should she run? Then she remembered what her parents had told her the summer before. "If you ever see a mountain lion," they had said, "stay as still as you can. Sudden moves could cause the lion to attack."

Elaine had stayed as still as she could. The lion had watched her for a moment, and then had begun to edge closer. At that moment, her mom and dad had rushed up. As they ran into the meadow, the lion turned and slipped away into the woods. That was when Elaine had collapsed into her father's arms.

Name ______________________________

Then What Happened? continued

Complete the sequence chart to show the order of events in the passage on page 49. Begin the chart with an event that happened the year before the events described in the passage.

Now go back to the passage and underline the sentences that tell where two different events happened at the same time. Circle the sequence words that helped you to figure this out.

Name ______________________________

Prefix Clues

Underline the word in each sentence that has the prefix *un-* or *re-*. Then write a meaning for the word on the line below the sentence.

Prefix	Meaning
un-	not
re-	again, back, backward

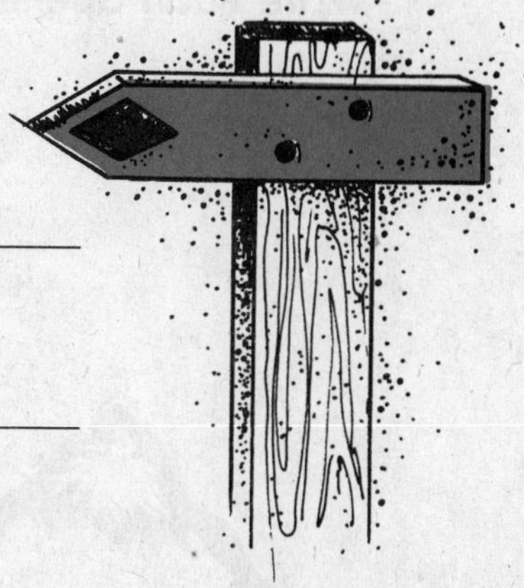

1. The hikers agreed to reassemble at the summit.

____

2. Some of them were unprepared for such a long hike.

____

3. They reconsidered their plan and turned back.

____

4. Jake felt unsteady on the narrow ledge.

____

5. He had renewed energy after eating a banana.

____

6. Danielle rearranged the contents of her bag, looking for the map.

____

7. Only when the bag was completely unpacked did she find the map.

____

8. When they reexamined the map, they saw that they did not have far to go.

____

9. Since the day was clear, they had an unobscured view of the valley.

____

10. Despite the unusually warm weather, it was cold on the summit.

____

Name ______________________

More Vowel Spellings

Remember these less common spellings for some long and short vowel sounds:

/ē/ *i*-consonant-*e* (rout**ine**) /ī/ *y* (c**y**cle)

/ĕ/ *ea* (sw**ea**t) /ĭ/ *y* (rh**y**thm) /ŭ/ *o*-consonant-*e* (sh**ove**)

Write each Spelling Word under its vowel sound.

Spelling Words

1. cycle
2. sweat
3. rhythm
4. rely
5. pleasant
6. routine
7. cleanse
8. shove
9. reply
10. meant
11. sponge
12. apply
13. threat
14. myth
15. deny
16. leather
17. rhyme
18. thread
19. meadow
20. ravine

Name ______________________________

Spelling Spree

Spelling Words

1. cycle
2. sweat
3. rhythm
4. rely
5. pleasant
6. routine
7. cleanse
8. shove
9. reply
10. meant
11. sponge
12. apply
13. threat
14. myth
15. deny
16. leather
17. rhyme
18. thread
19. meadow
20. ravine

Word Changes Write a Spelling Word to fit each clue.

1. Drop two letters from *really* to write a word meaning "to depend."
2. Change a letter in *moth* to write a synonym for *legend.*
3. Drop a consonant from *shovel* to write a word meaning "to push."
4. Replace a consonant in *great* with two letters to write a synonym for *danger.*
5. Change a letter in *repay* to write a synonym for *respond.*
6. Replace two letters in *circle* with one to write a shorthand word for riding a bike.
7. Add a consonant to *peasant* to write a word meaning "enjoyable."
8. Replace a consonant in *leader* with two letters to write a word that names a clothing material.

1. ______________ 5. ______________

2. ______________ 6. ______________

3. ______________ 7. ______________

4. ______________ 8. ______________

Word Addition Write a Spelling Word by adding the beginning of the first word to the end of the second word.

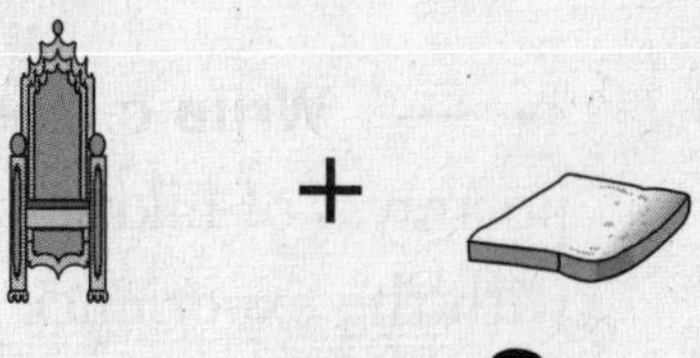

9. throne + bread = ______________
10. deal + funny = ______________
11. approach + fly = ______________
12. swing + defeat = ______________
13. rat + thyme = ______________
14. spoke + range = ______________

Name ______________________________

Proofreading and Writing

Proofreading Circle the six misspelled Spelling Words in this travel poster. Then write each word correctly.

You Need a Vacation!

Get away from the daily routeen and head for the mountains! You will clenz your body and your mind with a week of restful hiking and climbing. Follow well-marked trails to a pleasant meddow. Test your climbing skills as you explore a scenic ravene. Delight in the beauty and rythm of nature. You'll discover that the mountains are the place you were ment to be!

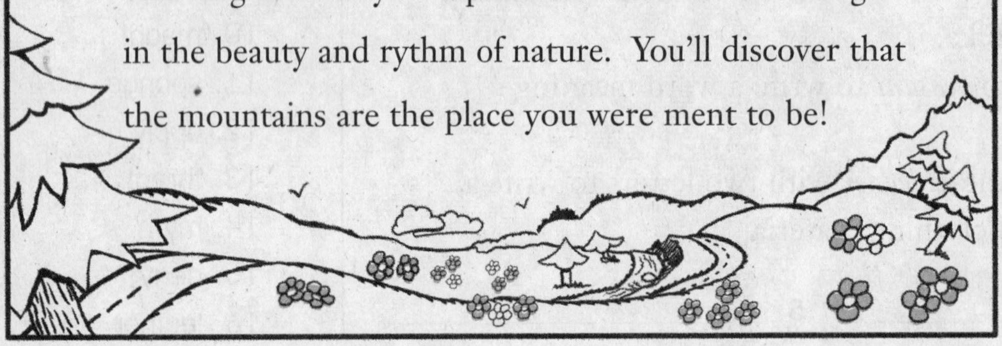

1. ______________
2. ______________
3. ______________
4. ______________
5. ______________
6. ______________

Spelling Words

1. cycle
2. sweat
3. rhythm
4. rely
5. pleasant
6. routine
7. cleanse
8. shove
9. reply
10. meant
11. sponge
12. apply
13. threat
14. myth
15. deny
16. leather
17. rhyme
18. thread
19. meadow
20. ravine

Write a Comparison and Contrast How does the portrayal of hiking and climbing in the poster above compare with the experience that Danielle and Jake had in the selection? Is one more realistic than the other? Is there anything missing from both accounts?

On a separate piece of paper, write a paragraph in which you compare and contrast the two descriptions. Use Spelling Words from the list.

Name ______________________

Dictionary Deciphering

Read the dictionary entries. Follow each numbered instruction.

des•o•late (dĕs′ ə lĭt) *adj.* Having few or no inhabitants; deserted: *an abandoned shack on a desolate road.* —*v.* **(dĕs′ ə lāt′).** *des•o•lat•ed, des•o•lat•ing, des•o•lates.* To make lonely, forlorn, or wretched: *The loss of our old dog desolated us.* **—des′o•late•ly** *adv.*

im•pro•vise (ĭm′ prə vīz′) *v.* **im•pro•vised, im•pro•vis•ing, im•pro•vis•es. 1.** To invent or perform without preparation: *The comics improvised several scenes based on audience suggestions.* **2.** To make on the spur of the moment from materials found nearby: *The hikers improvised a bridge out of fallen logs.* **—im′pro•vis′•er** *n.*

stag•ger (stăg′ ər) *v.* **stag•gered, stag•ger•ing, stag•gers. 1.** To move or stand unsteadily; totter. **2.** To begin to lose confidence or sense of purpose; waver.

tex•ture (tĕks′ chər) *n.* **1.** The structure of the interwoven threads or strands of a fabric: *Burlap has a coarse texture.* **2.** The appearance and feel of a surface: *The plaster gives the wall a rough texture.*

1. Write a sample sentence for the first definition of *stagger*.

   ____

2. Write a sentence using the noun *improviser.*

   ____

3. Write a sentence using the second definition of *texture.*

   ____

4. Write a sentence using the adjective *desolate.*

   ____

Name ______________________

After I Prepared, I Climbed the Mountain

Complex Sentences A clause contains both a subject and a predicate. An independent clause can stand by itself as a sentence. A subordinate clause cannot stand by itself as a sentence. A **complex sentence** has at least one subordinate clause and one independent clause.

A subordinate clause contains a subordinating conjunction. Here are some subordinating conjunctions:

after	because	since	when
although	before	unless	whenever
as	if	until	while

Join the two sentences using the subordinating conjunction shown in parentheses. Write the new complex sentence on the line.

1. You should not try to climb a mountain. You have prepared properly. (until)

____

2. They begin climbing. Skilled climbers check their equipment. (before)

____

3. They reached the peak. They enjoyed the view. (when)

____

4. Danielle and Jack reached their goal. They could improvise. (because)

____

5. I want to visit the weather station. I climb Mount Washington. (if)

____

Name ______________________________

Before I Climbed

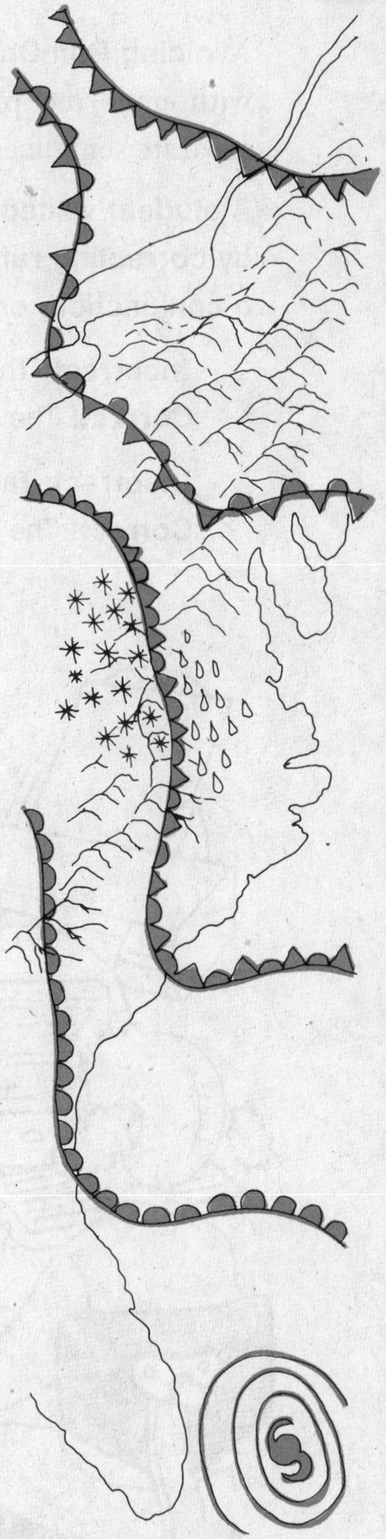

Correcting Fragments A **sentence fragment** does not express a complete thought. Correct a fragment by adding a subject or a predicate or both.

A **run-on sentence** expresses too many thoughts without correct punctuation. Correct a run-on sentence by creating separate sentences, a compound sentence, or a complex sentence.

Read the following sentence fragments or run-on sentences. Correct the problem, and write a new sentence on the line. There is more than one way to fix each sentence.

1. Because the weather can change quickly.

____

____

2. Meteorologists predict the daily weather, they make long-range forecasts.

____

____

3. This weather station has recorded the highest wind speeds. And the coldest temperatures in the state.

____

____

4. Visitors learn how a barometer works they get a tour of the weather station.

____

____

5. When the next storm comes.

____

____

Name ____________________

Will It Rain?

Avoiding Run-Ons A **run-on sentence** expresses too many thoughts without correct punctuation. Correct a run-on sentence by creating separate sentences, a compound sentence, or a complex sentence.

A student visited a weather station and wrote the following. Revise it by correcting run-on sentences. You might need to add punctuation, a conjunction, or both. Here are two examples:

Incorrect: The sky is cloudy I think it will rain.
Correct: The sky is cloudy. I think it will rain.

Incorrect: The sun came out it was still cold.
Correct: The sun came out, **but** it was still cold.

I want to be a weather forecaster someday ^ a big storm would be exciting. A snowstorm can cause traffic accidents ^ high winds can bring down power lines. I would want to be accurate ^ an accurate forecast helps people prepare for bad weather. I might be a scientist at a weather station ^ I might work at a television station. Because I want to be a weather scientist ^ I will study science.

Name ______________________________

Writing a Friendly Letter

A **friendly letter** is a letter that you write to a friend to share news about what is happening in your life.

Use this page to help you plan and organize a friendly letter. Either write a letter that Jake or Danielle might have written to a friend about climbing to the Mount Remington weather station, or write a letter to a friend of yours in which you share a recent experience or adventure of your own. Follow these steps:

1. Write a **heading** (your address and the date) and a **greeting** (*Dear* and the person's name followed by a comma).
2. Write the **body** of your letter below the greeting. Begin by writing something that shows you care about the friend to whom you are writing. At the end of the letter, ask your friend to write back soon.
3. Write an informal **closing** such as *Love* or *Your friend* followed by a comma in the lower right corner. Then sign your name under the closing.

Heading ______________________________

____

____

Greeting ______________________________

Body ______________________________

____

____

____

____

Closing ______________________________

Signature ______________________________

When you finish your friendly letter, copy it onto a clean sheet of paper. If you wrote your letter to a friend, address an envelope and mail it!

Name ______________________________

Voice

Every writer has a **voice**, or a unique way of saying things. This voice reflects the writer's personality and manner of expression. You can express your own personal voice in writing by using the following techniques:

- Make what you say sound like you.
- Include expressions and figures of speech you might use when speaking. When Danielle reaches the summit of Mount Remington and does not see the weather station, for example, she tells Jake "We're dead" to express her feelings of hopelessness.
- Write in a way that reflects your thoughts and feelings.

Think about how you express yourself in different situations. What do you usually say if you are upset or frustrated? On the lines below, write expressions and figures of speech that you might use to convey different feelings.

My Personal List of Expressions and Figures of Speech

______________________ (to express fear)	______________________ (to express worry)
______________________ (to express relief)	______________________ (to express confusion)
______________________ (to express joy)	______________________ (to express surprise)
______________________ (to express doubt)	______________________ (to express helplessness)
______________________ (to express sympathy)	______________________ (to express excitement)

When you revise your friendly letter, use several of these expressions and figures of speech to reflect your personal voice. By adding some of these expressions, you can make what you say sound more like you — as if you are speaking directly to your friend.

Name ______________________________

A Test of Courage

Use these words to complete the sentences below.

Vocabulary

ascent
entangled
seasoned
endeavored
rigging
ratlines
treacherous

1. Are you a ______________________ sailor, or is this your first voyage?
2. To prove that you will be an able sailor, you must climb to the top of the ______________________.
3. To start your climb, grab one of the ________________, the small ropes that form a ladder.
4. As you continue your ______________________ upward, be careful not to become entangled in the ropes.
5. Rain and wind make the climb even more ________________ than it usually is.
6. I have ______________________ to give you guidance, but you must find courage within yourself to make the climb.

Use two vocabulary words in a short description of what it might feel like to make the climb described above.

____

____

____

Name ______________________________

Predictions Chart

selection details + personal knowledge + THINKING = prediction

Selection Details page 99

► Charlotte must climb the tallest mast to prove her worth.

____

____

Personal Knowledge

____

____

____

Prediction: ______________________________

Selection Details page 105

► Charlotte makes it to just below the top gallant spar.

____

____

Personal Knowledge

____

____

____

Prediction: ______________________________

Selection Details page 107

► Charlotte begins her climb down.

____

____

Personal Knowledge

____

____

____

Prediction: ______________________________

Selection Details page 105

► Captain Jaggery appears on deck.

____

____

Personal Knowledge

____

____

____

Prediction: ______________________________

Name ______________________

A Day on the *Seahawk*

Answer the questions about the setting, characters, and plot of *The True Confessions of Charlotte Doyle*.

1. Where is Charlotte when the story begins?

____

2. What does she have to do to become a member of the crew?

____

3. Why doesn't Charlotte start over again after she realizes she has begun to climb the wrong set of rigging?

____

4. After the ship dips, how does Charlotte feel about her decision to climb?

____

5. How long does it take Charlotte to climb to a point on the mast that a seasoned sailor could reach in two minutes?

____

6. Why is climbing near the top of the mast more difficult than climbing closer to the bottom?

____

7. Why is climbing down the rigging more difficult than climbing up?

____

8. How does the crew react when Charlotte finally returns safely to the deck?

____

Name ______________________

You Guessed It!

Read the story. Then complete the activity on page 65.

The Deep End

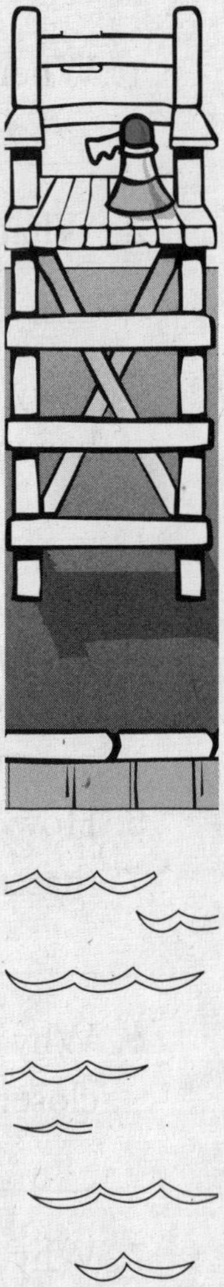

Manning flopped around in his bed like a fish. A moment before, he had been sinking to the bottom of a swimming pool. He heard muffled shouts coming from above. He flailed his arms, but it was no use. He just kept sinking. His father's voice roused him from his dream. "Are you ready for your first day of lifeguard training?" Manning groaned.

Rough and Ready Summer Camp was just about the only place around that gave summer jobs to teenagers younger than eighteen. Manning needed money for a backpacking trip to the Rocky Mountains in the fall. He needed to buy a train ticket to Montana. He needed a new backpack and new hiking boots. He needed a job!

He had applied for the position of assistant counselor. He got the job, but was then dismayed to find out that, like all counselors at the camp, he needed to go through lifeguard training. He was a capable swimmer, but he had one discomfort that had been with him all his life: he did not like to be in deep water. In fact, being in water over his head terrified him.

At ten o'clock training began at Taft Pool. The trainer announced that first they would take a swimming test—ten laps of freestyle. "When I blow my whistle, dive in and start swimming," he said. "This is not a race," he added, "it's a test of your endurance."

Manning's heart was pounding. He knew he'd be fine in the shallow water, but what would happen when he reached the deep end? "Swimmers, on your mark!" the trainer called. Manning got into diving position. At the shrill sound of the whistle, he took a deep breath and dove. His body hit the water smoothly, and he fell into an even stroke.

"Just breathe," he told himself as he swam toward the deep end. He concentrated on his stroke. To his relief, he didn't panic as he passed the five-foot marker on the side of the pool. Nor did he panic when he passed the eight-foot marker. By the time he reached the far side of the pool, he was just hitting his best rhythm. He flipped himself around and started back toward the shallow end.

Name ________________________________

You Guessed It! continued

Answer these questions about the passage on page 64.

1. Do you think Manning will successfully complete lifeguard training? Why or why not?

____

____

2. What information in the story might lead you to predict that Manning will not complete the training?

____

____

3. At which point in the story might you change your prediction?

____

____

4. What do you think Manning will do with the money he earns as assistant counselor?

____

____

5. The following statements are generally true in real life. Which statement helps you predict that Manning will most likely succeed in lifeguard training? Circle it.
   A. People often avoid what they fear.
   B. People will often face a difficult challenge to get something they really want.
   C. Good friends help each other through hard times.

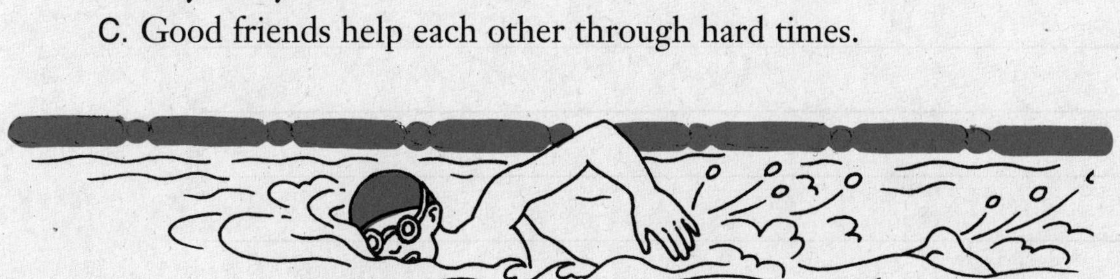

Name ____________________

Book Report Rewrite

Underline each contraction or possessive in this book report. Then, on the lines below, rewrite the report, replacing each contraction or possessive with its longer form.

The True Confessions of Charlotte Doyle
by Avi

Charlotte dresses in sailor's garb and asks to be accepted as a crew member. "You're a girl" is Dillingham's reply. "What'll the captain say?" Charlotte doesn't want to think about the task she must perform, but she's determined. Charlotte's climb is terrifying, but it's nothing compared to her descent. I'd highly recommend this book to adventure lovers. The book's author has also written many other entertaining stories.

Name ______________________________

The /ou/, /ŏŏ/, /ô/, and /oi/ Sounds

Remember these spelling patterns for the /ou/, the /ŏŏ /, the /ô/, and the /oi/ sounds:

/ou/ *ou* st**ou**t

/ŏŏ / *oo* bl**oo**m

/ô/ *au, aw, ough, augh* v**au**lt, squ**aw**k, s**ough**t, n**augh**ty

/oi/ *oi, oy* av**oi**d, ann**oy**

Write each Spelling Word under its vowel sound.

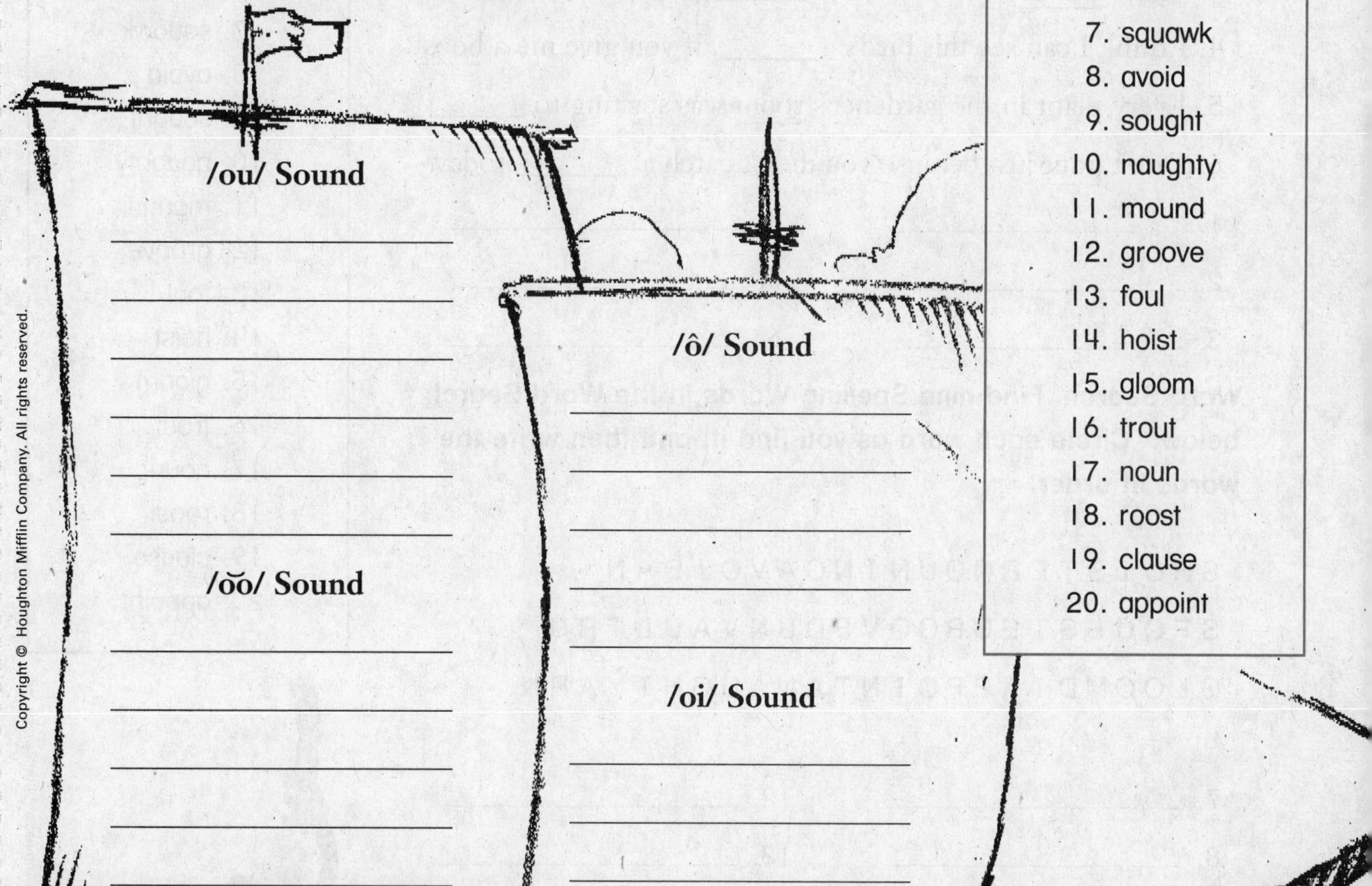

/ou/ Sound

____

____

____

____

____

/ŏŏ/ Sound

____

____

____

____

____

/ô/ Sound

____

____

____

____

____

/oi/ Sound

____

____

____

____

____

Spelling Words

1. bloom
2. stout
3. droop
4. crouch
5. annoy
6. vault
7. squawk
8. avoid
9. sought
10. naughty
11. mound
12. groove
13. foul
14. hoist
15. gloom
16. trout
17. noun
18. roost
19. clause
20. appoint

The True Confessions of Charlotte Doyle

Spelling The /ou/, /o͞o/, /ô/, and /oi/ Sounds

Name ______________________________

Spelling Spree

Find a Rhyme **Write a Spelling Word that rhymes with the underlined word.**

1. If you _______ down, you can see the kangaroo's <u>pouch</u>.
2. The baseball player <u>found</u> his glove near the pitcher's _______.
3. Please <u>pause</u> while I find the _______ in this sentence.
4. I think I can see this bird's _______, if you give me a <u>boost</u>.
5. Every plant in the gardener's <u>room</u> was starting to _______.
6. Don't <u>pout</u> just because you didn't catch a _______ today.

1. ______________ 4. ______________
2. ______________ 5. ______________
3. ______________ 6. ______________

Word Search **Find nine Spelling Words in the Word Search below. Circle each word as you find it, and then write the words in order.**

S H O I S T E R N O U N I N G A V O I D A N

S F O U L S T E G R O O V E D U N V A U L T R U

G L O O M D I A P P O I N T A N A U G H T Y A R N

7. ______________ 12. ______________
8. ______________ 13. ______________
9. ______________ 14. ______________
10. ______________ 15. ______________
11. ______________

Spelling Words

1. bloom
2. stout
3. droop
4. crouch
5. annoy
6. vault
7. squawk
8. avoid
9. sought
10. naughty
11. mound
12. groove
13. foul
14. hoist
15. gloom
16. trout
17. noun
18. roost
19. clause
20. appoint

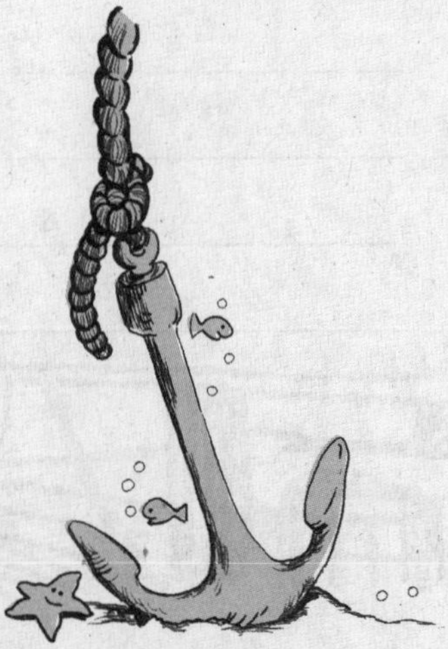

Name ________________________________

Proofreading and Writing

Proofreading **Circle the five misspelled Spelling Words in this part of a letter. Then write each word correctly.**

Dear Mother,

A most unusual event took place onboard today. Miss Charlotte Doyle, a young woman who saught to join the crew, managed to hoist herself to the top of the royal yard. Many of the crew had expected her to fail, and her success seemed to anoy more than a few of them. One sailor's response was to let his shoulders droup noticeably. Another let loose a rude squak and said, "She was just lucky." Personally, I think Miss Doyle has a stowt heart and will be a valuable addition to the ship.

1. ____________
2. ____________
3. ____________
4. ____________
5. ____________

Spelling Words

1. bloom
2. stout
3. droop
4. crouch
5. annoy
6. vault
7. squawk
8. avoid
9. sought
10. naughty
11. mound
12. groove
13. foul
14. hoist
15. gloom
16. trout
17. noun
18. roost
19. clause
20. appoint

Write a Character Sketch What does Charlotte Doyle's behavior tell you about her? What do you think about her ability to make herself climb to the top of the royal yard?

On a separate piece of paper, write a character sketch in which you describe Charlotte. Use Spelling Words from the list.

Name ______________________________

Word Family Matters

Decide which word best completes each sentence. Write the word in the blank.

1. The puppy barked ______________________ when our older dog was let out at night.
2. My ______________________ to you is to hike with a friend.
3. I hope you ______________________ your school vacation.
4. I don't ______________________ eat six cookies at lunchtime.
5. Why does my brother ______________________ everything I say?

Now write a sentence using two words you haven't used yet.

____

____

Vocabulary

joyous
rejoice
enjoy

advice
advise
adviser

opposite
oppose
opposition

horror
horribly
horrify

normal
normally
normalize

Name ______________________________

Charlotte and the Navy

Common and Proper Nouns A **common noun** names a person, a place, a thing, or an idea. A **proper noun** names a particular person, place, thing, or idea. Each important word in a proper noun is capitalized.

Determine which nouns in the following sentences are proper nouns and which are common nouns. List the nouns in the proper columns below the sentences.

Example: New Mexico is a state in the United States.

Proper Nouns	**Common Nouns**
New Mexico	state
United States	

1. Charlotte Doyle wanted to be a sailor.
2. My big sister joined the U.S. Navy.
3. Her ship is called *The Piedmont*.
4. Last year, she sailed to Hawaii.
5. The crew is sailing in the Atlantic Ocean now.

Proper Nouns	**Common Nouns**
______________________	______________________
______________________	______________________
______________________	______________________
______________________	______________________
______________________	______________________

Name ______________________________

Foxes and Deer

Singular and Plural Nouns A **singular noun** names one person, place, thing, or idea. A **plural noun** names more than one person, place, thing, or idea. To form the plural of most nouns, simply add *-s* or *-es* to the singular form. Some nouns have the same singular and plural forms, and some nouns have unusual plural forms. Study the examples below.

Singular	Plural	Singular	Plural
ship	ship**s**	chur**ch**	church**es**
walt**z**	waltz**es**	d**ay**	day**s**
Jone**s**	Jones**es**	di**sh**	dish**es**
sol**o**	solo**s**	scar**f**	scar**ves**
bo**ss**	boss**es**	fo**x**	fox**es**
count**y**	count**ies**	deer	**deer**

Compare the spelling pattern of each singular noun below to the ones in the list above. Then write the correct plural form. You may use a dictionary.

Singular	Plural
1. box	______________
2. city	______________
3. toss	______________
4. leaf	______________
5. watch	______________
6. cap	______________
7. ash	______________
8. yes	______________
9. zoo	______________
10. toy	______________

Name ______________________________

Ms. Doyle and President Kim

Capitalization and Punctuation of People's Titles A title before a person's name is capitalized. When a title is abbreviated, it is followed by a period.

Examples: I will introduce **Ms.** Clara Kindowsky.
The press interviewed **President** Carter.

Rewrite each sentence below. Use correct punctuation and capitalization for titles.

1. The sailors saluted captain Smith and lieutenant Lee.

____

____

2. A member of the crew approached Capt Smith and dr. Tilton.

____

____

3. Dr Tilton visited ensign Johnson, who was sick.

____

____

4. I recommend either mr. Kim or Mrs Ortiz for the position.

____

____

5. Mrs Ellison and principal Lesnikoski stood in the hallway.

____

____

Name ______________________________

Writing an Opinion Paragraph

An **opinion** is a strong belief or conclusion that may or may not be supported by facts and reasons. For example, Zachariah in *The True Confessions of Charlotte Doyle* expresses his opinion of Charlotte, saying, "You're as steady a girl as ever I've met." As you read a story, you will form your own opinions about its characters.

As you read *The True Confessions of Charlotte Doyle,* think about this question: *Do you think Charlotte should have been allowed to prove her competence as a sailor by climbing to the top of the royal yard, or should someone have stopped her from performing this hazardous feat?*

Then use this diagram to record your opinion and to write facts and examples that support it.

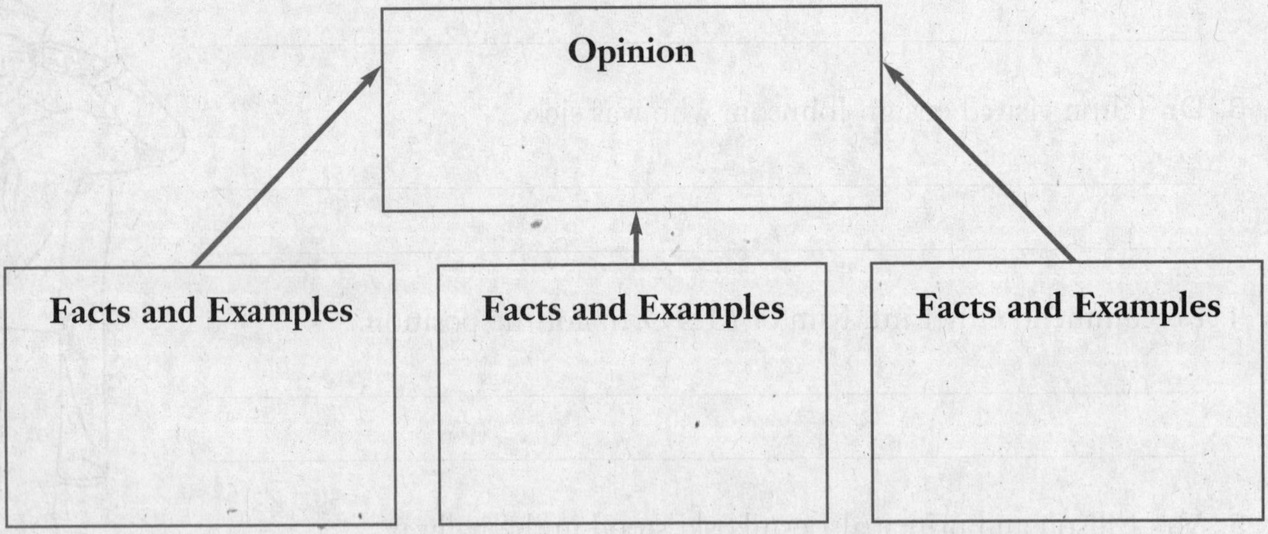

Using the information you recorded in the diagram, write an opinion paragraph on a separate sheet of paper. In the first sentence, state your opinion in response to the question above. In the body of the paragraph, write two to three reasons why you think and feel the way you do. Support your opinion with facts and examples. Then end your paragraph with a concluding sentence that restates your opinion.

Name ______________________________

Combining Sentences with Appositives

One way to improve your writing is to combine two short sentences into one by using an appositive. An **appositive** is a word or group of words that immediately follows a noun and identifies or explains it. Appositives are usually set off from the rest of the sentence by commas. Here is an example of before and after:

Charlotte Doyle was a thirteen-year-old girl. She joined the crew of the *Seahawk*.

Charlotte Doyle**, a thirteen-year-old girl,** joined the crew of the *Seahawk*.

Revise the following sentences from Captain Jaggery's ship's log. Combine each pair of short, choppy sentences into a single sentence with an appositive.

Charlotte Doyle is a young passenger. She wants to work aboard the Seahawk.

____

Today two members of the crew described a test of worth that Charlotte had to pass. Zachariah and Foley are the crew members who described the test.

____

____

The men asked Charlotte to climb to the top of the royal yard. The royal yard is the tallest mast of the ship.

____

____

Ewing gave Charlotte some helpful advice. He is a seasoned sailor.

____

Happily, Charlotte passed the test with flying colors. The test was a difficult physical and mental challenge.

____

____

Name ______________________________

Words for Change

Write the letter to match each word with its definition.

_____ boycott
_____ petition
_____ reproach
_____ activists
_____ segregation
_____ civil rights

a. people who work hard for a cause they believe in
b. separating people by race
c. the rights belonging to a citizen
d. disapproval
e. a document that requests something
f. a protest that involves refusing to deal with a certain business or person

Write a sentence for each vocabulary word in the spaces provided.

1. activists: ______________________________
2. petition: ______________________________
3. boycott: ______________________________
4. reproach: ______________________________
5. segregation: ______________________________
6. civil rights: ______________________________

Name ______________________________

Making a Difference

After reading each selection, complete the chart below to show what you learned.

	Rosa Parks: My Story 	*Making a Difference* 
What challenge does the main character face?		
Details that show the main character's courage	1. 2.	1. 2.

Name ______________________________

Compare and Contrast Judgments

In *Rosa Parks: My Story,* what beliefs and opinions mattered deeply to Rosa Parks? Choose one quotation to copy into the chart below. Make a judgment about that belief or opinion. In the second block indicate on a scale of 1 (strongly disagree) to 10 (strongly agree) whether you agree with the statement or not. In the third block give at least one reason to support your judgment. Sample answers are provided. Then fill out the next column of the chart using a quotation from another selection in this theme.

	Selection Title: ***Rosa Parks: My Story***	**Selection Title:** ______________
Quotation That States an Opinion or Belief		
Check Scale	**Disagree** ______________ **Agree**	**Disagree** ______________ **Agree**
Supporting Reason		

Monitoring Student Progress

Key Vocabulary

Name ______________________________

Outdoor Words

Use the words from the box to complete the sentences below.

Vocabulary

- frantic
- fluttering
- stealthily
- lunged
- biodegradable

1. "Make sure to throw your cups in the trash can," Mrs. Newsom said. "Plastic is not a ______________ substance."
2. The cat crept ______________ toward the unsuspecting robin.
3. The robin escaped, ______________ its wings as it flew off.
4. Andy ______________ forward as he tried to catch a butterfly in his net.
5. A rabbit tangled in a piece of wire hopped back and forth, ______________ to get loose.

Use at least two vocabulary words in a short description of what it might be like to spend a day cleaning up a park, lake, or other natural area.

____

____

____

____

Name ______________________________

Test Practice

Use the three steps you've learned to choose the best answer for these questions about *Making a Difference.* Fill in the circle for the best answer in the answer row at the bottom of the page.

1. What is the main idea of *Making a Difference?*

A A girl has a picnic on her favorite island.

B A girl inspires her classmates with a speech.

C A girl helps her sister free a pelican.

D A girl fears speaking in front of others.

2. Where does the first part of *Making a Difference* take place?

F on an island

G in a boat

H in a classroom

J near a picnic table

3. Why do you think the pelican lunges at Elena but not at Gloria?

A Elena walks loudly but Gloria walks quietly.

B Elena tries to take the string off the bird while Gloria takes the string off the roots.

C Elena screams "Ay!" but Gloria speaks softly.

D Elena accidentally hits the bird with a stick, but Gloria strokes its head.

4. **Connecting/Comparing** Think about *Making a Difference* and *Hatchet.* In what way are Gloria and Brian alike?

F Both work with others to improve the environment.

G Both help others by their actions.

H Both are stranded in the wilderness.

J Both bravely face their fears.

ANSWER ROWS		
	1 Ⓐ Ⓑ Ⓒ Ⓓ	3 Ⓐ Ⓑ Ⓒ Ⓓ
	2 Ⓕ Ⓖ Ⓗ Ⓙ	4 Ⓕ Ⓖ Ⓗ Ⓙ

Continue on page 82.

Name ______________________________

Test Practice continued

5. Why does Gloria give the first speech?
   - **A** Ms. Acosta asks Gloria to go first.
   - **B** Gloria feels that she has something important to say.
   - **C** Gloria wants to get the speech over fast.
   - **D** Gloria's classmates ask her to go first.

6. What is one result of Gloria's speech?
   - **F** Gloria's classmates want to help her clean up the island.
   - **G** Gloria learns that no one cares about brown pelicans.
   - **H** Gloria decides to give more speeches about saving wildlife.
   - **J** Gloria's teacher gives her an A+ for the speech.

7. What was the author's purpose in writing *Making a Difference*?
   - **A** to tell a story about a brave girl who inspired others to act
   - **B** to give information about students who work to protect wildlife
   - **C** to convince people who fish not to use fishing line
   - **D** to suggest topics for speeches about wildlife

8. **Connecting/Comparing** In what way is Gloria like Danielle in *Climb or Die*?
   - **F** Gloria gives up on trying to solve a problem.
   - **G** Gloria argues with a family member about a solution.
   - **H** Gloria figures out how to solve a serious problem.
   - **J** Gloria describes a problem and her solution to her classmates.

ANSWER ROWS		
	5 Ⓐ Ⓑ Ⓒ Ⓓ	7 Ⓐ Ⓑ Ⓒ Ⓓ
	6 Ⓕ Ⓖ Ⓗ Ⓙ	8 Ⓕ Ⓖ Ⓗ Ⓙ

Monitoring Student Progress

Comprehension Skill Making Judgments

Name ______________________

What Do You Think?

Read the details below about Rosa Parks and the important actions she took. Then answer the questions.

- Rosa Parks didn't join those who took a petition to the bus company and city officials.
- She didn't want to ask anyone for favors.
- She made decisions herself, as an individual.
- She didn't sit in the bus seat with the intention of getting arrested.
- She remained in the bus seat because she was tired of giving in.

1. What does her decision not to give up her seat on the bus tell you about Rosa Parks? Make three judgements about Rosa Parks' personality.

____

____

____

____

____

2. Explain why you believe your judgements about Rosa Parks to be true. Use details from the selection.

____

____

____

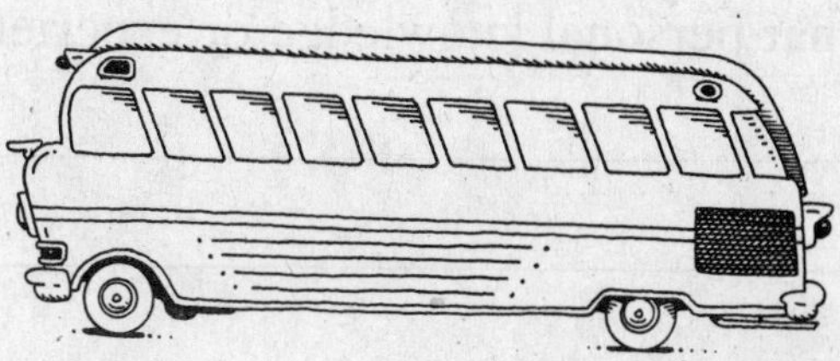

Name ______________________________

What Would They Do If...?

Read each situation below and answer the questions that follow it. Look in the Anthology if you need help remembering details.

Situation 1: Think about *Making a Difference* on Anthology pages 116H–116L. Imagine that Gloria finds out that a seal at a nearby beach was injured after it swallowed the type of plastic holder that holds six cans of soft-drinks.

1. How do you predict Gloria might react?

____

2. What story details helped you make this prediction?

____

____

3. What personal knowledge or experiences helped you with your prediction?

____

Situation 2: Think about *Climb or Die* on Anthology pages 74–86. Imagine that Danielle and Jake discover that the men at the weather station cannot help them and that the nearest town is on the other side of Mount Remington.

4. What do you predict Jake and Danielle might do?

____

____

5. What story details helped you make this prediction?

____

____

6. What personal knowledge or experiences helped you with your prediction?

____

____

Name ______________________________

Monitoring Student Progress

Structural Analysis
Syllabication

Word Division Decision

Read each sentence. Rewrite each underlined word with slashes to divide the syllables.

1. The <u>pilot</u> kept the little plane on a <u>steady</u> course.
   ____
2. The wind <u>buffeted</u> the plane a bit as it dropped in <u>altitude</u>.
   ____
3. Annie had <u>taken</u> the seat <u>closest</u> to the window.
   ____
4. She watched as seven brown pelicans <u>glided</u> below with <u>outspread</u> wings.
   ____
5. The <u>ungainly</u> birds flew in a V <u>formation</u>.
   ____
6. The birds quickly <u>vanished</u> in the <u>distance</u>.
   ____
7. Annie <u>wondered</u> how far they might <u>travel</u>.
   ____
8. Then she noticed a <u>passenger</u> ship on the <u>horizon</u>.
   ____
9. Annie's <u>secret</u> dream was to become a cruise ship <u>captain</u>.
   ____

Name ______________________________

Monitoring Student Progress

Vocabulary Skill Using Dictionary Entries

Identifying Dictionary Entries

Choose the correct label for each part of the dictionary entry. Write the labels in the spaces provided.

adjectival form	part of speech
adverbial form	pronunciation
entry word	sample sentence or phrase
first definition	second definition

____

____

____

____

numb (nŭm) *adj.* **-er, -est 1.** Deprived of the power to feel or move normally. *My fingers were numb with cold.* **2.** Stunned or paralyzed, as from shock. *He was numb from the terrible news.* **—numbly** *adv.* **—numbness** *n.*

____

____

____

____

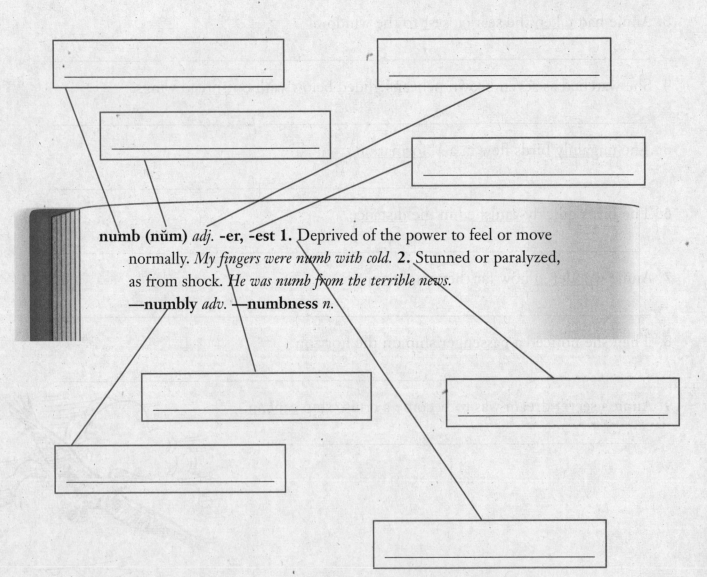

Name ______________________________

Spelling Review

Write Spelling Words from the list to answer the questions.

1–8. Which eight words have the /ă/, /ĕ/, /ĭ/, /ŏ/, or /ŭ/ sound?

1. ____________ 5. ____________
2. ____________ 6. ____________
3. ____________ 7. ____________
4. ____________ 8. ____________

9–30. Which twenty-two words have the /ā/, /ē/, /ī/, /ō/, /yo͞o/, /ou/, /o͞o/, /ô/, or /oi/ sound?

9. ____________ 20. ____________
10. ____________ 21. ____________
11. ____________ 22. ____________
12. ____________ 23. ____________
13. ____________ 24. ____________
14. ____________ 25. ____________
15. ____________ 26. ____________
16. ____________ 27. ____________
17. ____________ 28. ____________
18. ____________ 29. ____________
19. ____________ 30. ____________

Spelling Words

1. ravine
2. wince
3. squawk
4. gaze
5. league
6. vault
7. bulk
8. avoid
9. theme
10. sought
11. depth
12. throne
13. hoist
14. strive
15. routine
16. prompt
17. stout
18. mute
19. reply
20. strain
21. roam
22. meant
23. annoy
24. craft
25. naughty
26. rhythm
27. sponge
28. sleeve
29. foul
30. bloom

Name ______________________

Spelling Spree

Puzzle Play **Write a Spelling Word to fit each clue.**

1. a plant's flower ☐ ___ ___ ___ ___ ___
2. a muscle injury ___ ___ ☐ ___ ___ ___
3. screech ___ ___ ___ ☐ ___ ___
4. a jacket's arm covering ___ ___ ___ ___ ☐ ___
5. a steady look ___ ___ ___ ☐
6. a recurring pattern of sound or movement ☐ ___ ___ ___ ___ ___
7. disobedient ___ ___ ___ ___ ___ ___ ☐

Now write the boxed letters in order. They will spell a mystery word that is a synonym for *courage*.

Mystery Word: ☐☐☐☐☐☐☐

Spelling Words

1. vault
2. theme
3. sleeve
4. squawk
5. meant
6. throne
7. rhythm
8. stout
9. strain
10. hoist
11. sponge
12. bloom
13. naughty
14. annoy
15. gaze

Word Switch **Write a Spelling Word to replace each underlined word or word group in these sentences.**

8. The gold coins were kept in a locked storage area for valuables. ____________
9. The ruler's chair was inlaid with gems. ____________
10. Movers used a crane to haul up the piano to the top floor. ____________
11. We discussed the subject of the book. ____________
12. I intended to give her your message, but I forgot. ____________
13. The ship was tied to the dock with strong and sturdy ropes. ____________
14. The fly's constant buzzing began to irritate me. ____________
15. Please wipe off the table. ____________

Name ______________________________

Proofreading and Writing

Proofreading **Circle the six misspelled Spelling Words in this letter to the editor. Then write each word correctly.**

As a usual routene, I don't write letters to newspapers. (The bulck of my writing is reserved for homework!) I must, though, tell the public about a very special person.

Last Saturday, the weather was really fowle. Since my baseball leage practice was canceled, I decided to test my new hiking rain gear. In the hills near town, I slipped and fell into a deep gully. Gushing rainwater swept me along, and I was struck muete with terror! Suddenly, a stranger's arms grabbed me and began to hoist me to solid ground. I can never thank that person enough for my rescue. From now on, I will stryve to be as courageous as he is!

Spelling Words

1. bulk
2. mute
3. prompt
4. craft
5. league
6. avoid
7. roam
8. ravine
9. reply
10. foul
11. depth
12. routine
13. wince
14. sought
15. strive

1. ____________ 3. ____________ 5. ____________

2. ____________ 4. ____________ 6. ____________

Just the Opposite **Write the Spelling Word that means almost the opposite of each word or words.**

7. to grin ____________
8. stand still ____________
9. found ____________
10. hilltop ____________
11. width ____________
12. confront ____________
13. late ____________
14. lack of ability ____________
15. to ask ____________

Write an Interview Script **On a separate sheet of paper, write the script of an interview with a real or imagined hero. Use the Spelling Review Words.**

Name ______________________________

Monitoring
Student Progress

Grammar Skill Kinds of Sentences

Classifying and Rewriting Sentence Types

Write what kind of sentence each is—*declarative, interrogative, imperative,* or *exclamatory.*

1. Why was Rosa Parks arrested? ____________________
2. She challenged an unfair law. ____________________
3. How courageous she was! ____________________
4. Make a timeline of the civil rights movement. ____________________

Read the sentences. Rewrite each as the sentence type indicated in parentheses. Use correct end punctuation.

5. Did Ms. Parks work in Montgomery, Alabama? (declarative)

____

6. She was determined to eliminate segregation on city buses. (interrogative)

____

7. You should read this biography of Rosa Parks. (imperative)

____

8. Stories of heroism inspire me. (exclamatory)

____

Name ______________________________

Identifying and Writing Conjunctions and Compound Sentences

Circle each conjunction in the sentences below. After each compound sentence, write *compound sentence.*

1. Birds try to avoid humans, but sometimes they need some human help.

   ____

2. Sometimes a bird will get entangled in string or wire.

   ____

3. One helper must calm the bird, and the other must free it from the tangles.

   ____

Rewrite each pair of sentences as a compound sentence. Use correct end punctuation.

4. My brother saw a baby bird. He did not touch it.

   ____

5. It was in a nest. Its mother was nowhere around.

   ____

6. Soon the mother returned. We were glad we had left the baby bird alone.

   ____

Name ______________________________

Words About a Poem

Read the first stanza of a poem by Henry Wadsworth Longfellow. Then use words from the box to complete the statements about it.

Vocabulary

- figurative language
- lines
- repetition
- rhyme
- rhythm
- sensory language

The day is cold, and dark, and dreary;
It rains, and the wind is never weary;
The vine still clings to the moldering wall,
But at every gust the dead leaves fall,
And the day is dark and dreary.

1. There are five ______________________ in this stanza.
2. The poet uses ______________________ when he compares the wind to a person who is "never weary."
3. The beats of syllables suggest a heavy, sad, plodding ______________________.
4. The poet uses ______________________ by making the last line almost the same as the first line.
5. The poet ends the first pair of lines and the second pair of lines with ______________________.
6. Words such as *clings*, *gust*, *cold*, *dark*, and *moldering* help readers see, touch, and even smell the scene. The words are examples of ______________________.

Name ___________________________________

Literary Devices in Poetry

Device	Poem Title	Examples
Sensory Language: words that describe how things look, smell, feel, taste, and sound <u>Example:</u> *tiny pawprints in the wet sand*		
Figurative Language: imaginative comparisons between unlike things <u>Examples:</u> *a voice as calm as moonlight* (simile); *icicles were dripping fangs* (metaphor); *breezes danced playfully* (personification)		
Rhyme: similar end sounds <u>Examples:</u> *friend/end; pale/detail*		
Repetition: repeated use of words, phrases, or lines <u>Example:</u> *A happy bird/Am I, am I.*		

Name ______________________

Describing Poetry

Complete each statement about the poem indicated.

1. In the poem "Child Rest," the poet tells about

____

______________________.

An example of sensory language in the poem is

____

______________________.

2. In "Poem," the poet uses repetition when he says

____

______________________.

The poet may have decided to use repetition because

____

______________________.

3. In the poem "The People, Yes," the poet tells about

____

______________________.

An example of figurative language is

____

____

____

Name ______________________________

Comparing Poems

Choose two poems from this section. Compare and contrast them by answering the questions in the chart. Add questions of your own to the chart too.

	Poem #1 Title: ______________	**Poem #2** Title: ______________
What is the poet's main point?		
What words in the poem help you imagine and feel?		
Does the poem remind you of something from your own life? Explain.		
What is the mood or tone?		

Which poem did you like more? Why?

____

____

____

Name ____________________________

What Makes a Good Poem?

Reread the poem "Oranges" on pages 126–127. Fill in the blanks below to complete a summary of the story that the poem tells.

The narrator is a twelve-year-old boy who describes a time in December when he goes on his __________ with a girl. After he meets her at her house, they both walk to a __________. He brings her to the __________ and tells her to pick what she wants. She picks a chocolate that costs a __________ and he has only a __________. The boy then places the nickel and an orange from his pocket on the counter. Fortunately, the saleslady understands that the boy wants to __________ the girl but doesn't have the __________. After that, the boy and the girl walk __________.

Answer these questions. Include quotations from the poem. Sample answers given below. Try to use names of literary devices too.

1. How does the poet make the time of year come alive?

____

____

____

2. How does the poet show the narrator's feelings about the girl?

____

____

____

3. What is a particularly vivid image in the poem?

____

____

Name ______________________

Prefixes and Suffixes

The words in the box have the prefixes *re-* and *un-* and the suffixes *-less, -ful,* and *-ly.* Find the word that matches each clue. Write it in the letter spaces.

reunited	priceless	unaware	carelessly	plentiful
completely	unknown	fearfully	breathless	retelling

1. in a total way: ___ ___ ___ ___ ___ [___] ___ ___ ___ ___
2. without taking in air: ___ ___ ___ ___ ___ ___ [___] ___ ___ ___
3. not seeing or feeling something: ___ ___ ___ [___] ___ ___ ___
4. explaining again: ___ ___ [___] ___ ___ ___ ___ ___ ___
5. like a treasure: ___ ___ ___ ___ ___ ___ [___] ___ ___
6. more than enough: [___] ___ ___ ___ ___ ___ ___ ___ ___
7. together again: ___ [___] ___ ___ ___ ___ ___ ___
8. not at all bravely: ___ ___ [___] ___ ___ ___ ___ ___ ___
9. not familiar: ___ ___ [___] ___ ___ ___ ___
10. in a sloppy way: ___ ___ ___ ___ ___ ___ [___] ___ ___ ___

Write the boxed letters in order on the spaces below to complete the quotation.

An ancient Greek once wrote, "Painting is silent poetry, and poetry painting

___ ___ ___ ___   ___ ___ ___ ___ ___ ___."

Name ______________________________

Silent to Sounded

You can sometimes remember how to spell a word with a silent consonant by thinking of a related word in which the letter is pronounced.

silent consonant: sof<u>t</u>en
sounded consonant: sof<u>t</u>

Write a pair of related Spelling Words in each row. For each pair, underline the letter that is silent in one word and pronounced in the other.

Silent Consonant	Sounded Consonant

Spelling Words

1. autumn
2. autumnal
3. muscle
4. muscular
5. crumb
6. crumble
7. sign
8. signal
9. bomb
10. bombard
11. haste
12. hasten
13. column
14. columnist
15. heir
16. inherit
17. hymn
18. hymnal
19. design
20. designate

Name ______________________________

Spelling Spree

Analogies Complete each analogy. Write a Spelling Word so that the second pair of words has the same relationship as the first pair.

1. *Scream* is to *yell* as *hurry* is to __________.
2. *Tune* is to *melody* as *songbook* is to __________.
3. *Day* is to *Thursday* as *season* is to __________.
4. *Book* is to *novelist* as *newspaper* is to __________.
5. *Heavy* is to *light* as *flabby* is to __________.
6. *Wide* is to *narrow* as *row* is to __________.
7. *Save* is to *preserve* as *attack* is to __________.
8. *Poem* is to *haiku* as *song* is to __________.
9. *Dry* is to *moisten* as *stick* is to __________.

Spelling Words

1. autumn
2. autumnal
3. muscle
4. muscular
5. crumb
6. crumble
7. sign
8. signal
9. bomb
10. bombard
11. haste
12. hasten
13. column
14. columnist
15. heir
16. inherit
17. hymn
18. hymnal
19. design
20. designate

Phrase Fillers Write the Spelling Word that completes each phrase.

10. to clean up every __________
11. a __________ cramp
12. to __________ a representative
13. the saying that __________ makes waste
14. to __________ a fortune
15. to __________ for help

Name ____________________________________

Proofreading and Writing

Proofreading Circle the five misspelled Spelling Words in this poem. Then write each word correctly.

Of all the lovely seasons,
It's autumn Mom holds dear,
Bright colors splashed on every tree,
And days so cool and clear.
Leaves without haste dance to the ground,
An autunmal waltz that makes no sound.
As my mother's air, I must agree,
The leaves are a special sine,
Like the explosion of a huge paint bom,
A unique seasonal desine.

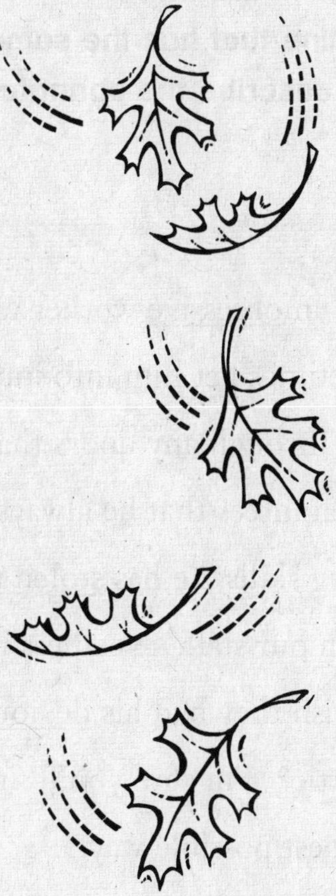

1. ____________________
2. ____________________
3. ____________________
4. ____________________
5. ____________________

Spelling Words

1. autumn
2. autumnal
3. muscle
4. muscular
5. crumb
6. crumble
7. sign
8. signal
9. bomb
10. bombard
11. haste
12. hasten
13. column
14. columnist
15. heir
16. inherit
17. hymn
18. hymnal
19. design
20. designate

Write an Opinion What kind of poems do you like best? Do you like funny poems or ones that touch your emotions? Do you prefer poems that rhyme or ones that have a free-flowing rhythm?

On a separate sheet of paper, write a paragraph that explains what kind of poems you like. Give reasons why you like that kind of poetry. Use Spelling Words from the list.

Name ______________________________

Negatives to Positives

Susie Plotkin thinks Artie is a great reporter, but the job recommendation she wrote for him doesn't sound very positive. Fix her letter by replacing each underlined word with one that has either a positive or a neutral connotation. Write the new word on the line that has the same number. Next to each word, write *positive* or *neutral* to describe the connotation of your new word.

Artie Shaw is an obsessive (1) worker who never leaves a job unfinished. His nosiness (2) can sometimes get him into impossible (3) situations, but he always manages to barge (4) through any doors that are slammed (5) in his face. His cutthroat (6) style guarantees that he always finishes first. Thanks to Artie's relentless (7) reporting skills, he has stolen (8) many lurid (9) stories from under the noses of other writers on our staff. Needless to say, his coworkers resent (10) him. If you ask me, they all wish they had his devious (11) talent for news gathering. What else can I say about Artie? I'm sure you'll find him a very odd (12) employee, and I mean that in the best possible way.

1. ______________________ 7. ______________________

2. ______________________ 8. ______________________

3. ______________________ 9. ______________________

4. ______________________ 10. ______________________

5. ______________________ 11. ______________________

6. ______________________ 12. ______________________

Name ______________________________

Apple Season

Using Subordinate Clauses Compound sentences can be changed into complex sentences, using subordinating conjunctions.

Rewrite each sentence as a complex sentence, using a subordinating conjunction from the box. Use each conjunction once. Use commas correctly.

after	as	before	when	while

1. The apples in Grandma Wallace's orchard ripen, and everyone in the family helps pick them.

____

____

2. The apples have been picked, and they must be washed.

____

____

3. Dad spreads newspaper on the floor, and the grandchildren begin peeling the apples.

____

____

4. Dad cuts each apple into pieces, and he also removes the core with its seeds.

____

____

5. The apples simmer slowly in a big pot, and Grandma occasionally stirs them.

____

____

Name ___________________________

Farewell to a Friend

Compound-Complex Sentences A compound sentence and a subordinate clause can be combined to form a compound-complex sentence.

Rewrite each pair of sentences as a compound-complex sentence, using a subordinating conjunction from the box. Use each conjunction once. Use commas correctly.

although	while	because	before	when

1. My best friend Jamie told us she was moving. I felt very sad, and we both cried.

____

____

2. Jamie's father has a new job. Her family will move to Idaho, and they plan to leave soon.

____

____

3. Jamie leaves next month. Our class will make a memory poster, and Jerome will write a funny poem for her.

____

____

4. We will miss Jamie. We hope she will be happy in her new school, and we want her to write to us.

____

____

5. We still have some time. She and I will go to some movies, and she will sleep over at my house.

____

____

Focus on Poetry

Grammar Skills Using Commas with Long Sentences

Name ____________________

Poetry in Motion

Using Commas with Long Sentences Use a comma before the conjunction to separate the two parts of a compound sentence. Use a comma after a subordinate clause when the clause begins a sentence. A comma is usually not used before a subordinate clause at the end of a sentence.

Use proofreading marks to correct the ten errors in punctuation and capitalization in this journal entry.

Example: before I walked, to the gym I went to my poetry class?

May 2

While I was playing basketball I had a terrific idea for a poem. The first part would have the rhythm of dribbling and the second part would have the soaring grace of a great leap when the game was over I dashed back to my locker. I grabbed my favorite pen with green ink and quickly wrote eight short lines. After I read those lines to myself I added two long lines, and, then I read the poem to my friend Anton. Anton said that I should submit my poem to the school newspaper because it was so clever. Who knows, maybe I'll be a published author?

Proofreading Marks

- Indent
- Add
- Delete
- Capital letter
- Small letter
- Add Period
- Add Comma
- Add Quotes
- Transpose

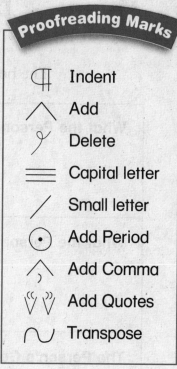

Name ______________________________

Planning a Poem About a Person

The person I have chosen is ______________.

What the Person Looks Like
What the Person Sounds Like
The Person's Gestures and Habits
Meaningful Things the Person Has Done
What the Person Likes and Dislikes
How I Feel About the Person

Name ______________________________

Sensory Language

Identify the sensory language in this passage.
Write the words and phrases on the chart in the correct space.

The Creative Chef

I could tell by the smoky odor and sizzling hiss that my brother Paul had invaded the kitchen. I walked in. A pot was spilling over with thick red sauce. On the counter was a pan heaped with drooping slices of eggplant. Paul smiled weakly. "Hi," he said. "I call this dish Eggplant Madness. It will be ready in an hour. I bet you can't wait to try some." Then he raced to the pot and stirred furiously. "Don't worry, I threw away the burned part. Here, taste this sauce."

I'm a sport. I took the spoon Paul offered and slid the warm, smooth sauce into my mouth. I recognized a zingy garlic flavor and a tinge of sweet basil. Believe it or not, I was starting to look forward to Eggplant Madness.

Sight	
Hearing	
Taste	
Smell	
Touch	

Write a sentence of your own that could belong in "The Creative Chef." Use sensory language.

____

____

Name ______________________________

What Really Happened?

Each selection in this theme attempts to explain a mystery. After reading each selection, complete the chart below and on the next page to show what you learned about these mysteries.

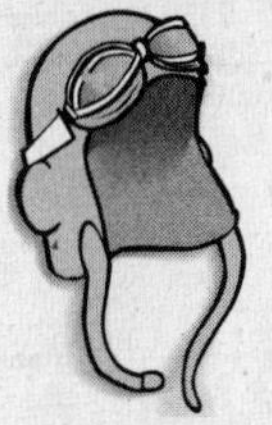

	Amelia Earhart: First Lady of Flight	The Girl Who Married the Moon	Dinosaur Ghosts
What mystery does the selection attempt to explain?			
What do you think the author's purpose was in writing the selection?			
What kind of writing is the selection an example of?			

Name ______________________

What Really Happened? continued

	Amelia Earhart: First Lady of Flight	The Girl Who Married the Moon	Dinosaur Ghosts
How did the author attempt to explain the mystery?			
Why do you think the mystery fascinates people?			

What are some different ways in which people try to explain mysterious events?

____

____

____

Name ______________________________

A Tragic Disappearance

Use these words to complete the paragraph below.

Vocabulary

- accounting
- journal
- runway
- disappearance
- aviation
- taxied
- inspiration
- accomplish
- navigator
- transmission

One of the greatest mysteries in the history of ______________ is the ______________ of famed pilot Amelia Earhart and her ______________ Fred Noonan. When Amelia ______________ down the ______________ and took off toward Howland Island on the second of July, 1937, she seemed certain to ______________ her goal of flying around the world at the equator. She had been giving an ______________ of her experiences to newspapers, and her words were an ______________ to millions of people everywhere. She was also keeping a ______________, in which she recorded her thoughts. During that day's flight, radio operators lost contact with Amelia after she sent a confusing ______________ over the radio. She and Noonan never reached their goal. It may never be known for sure what happened.

Name ______________________________

Fact and Opinion Chart

Passage	Fact or Opinion?	How I Can Tell
Page 148: She had read the note but believed Noonan had made an error.		
Page 148: Noonan had been right that it was necessary to turn south in order to get to Dakar.		
Page 151: Earhart's plane ran out of gas and crashed at sea.		
Page 152: Amelia Earhart was spying for the U.S. government.		
Page 153: The Japanese did not let the U.S. search party into their waters, or onto the islands they controlled, to look for Amelia and Fred.		
Page 154: When Goerner showed the islanders photographs of several women, all of them picked Earhart as the woman they had seen.		
Page 154: Amelia had been brainwashed and was "Tokyo Rose."		
Page 156: Amelia was "a tragedy of the sea."		

Name ______________________________

Mystery Fact Sheet

Fill in the fact sheet below with important information from the selection.

The pilot: ______________________

The navigator: ______________________

The goal: ______________________

Where their plane disappeared: ______________________

____

What Happened?

The Theories	Supporting Evidence	Evidence Against
1. They ran out of gas and crashed into the ocean.		
2. They were spies for the United States.		
3. Amelia was still alive.		
4. Amelia crashed on Nikumaroro.		

Name ______________________________

Focus on Facts

Read the passage. Then complete the activity on page 115.

Jacqueline Cochran, American Aviator

Jacqueline Cochran was a record-breaking female aviator. Though not as famous as Charles Lindbergh or Amelia Earhart, she certainly deserves to be.

Jacqueline was born in the early 1900s in Pensacola, Florida. She had a poor childhood in a lumber mill town. By age thirteen, she was working as a hair cutter in a beauty salon. Eventually, she moved to New York City and started her own cosmetics company. This was a courageous and admirable achievement. So that she could sell her products in more places, she learned to fly. "At that moment, when I paid for my first lesson," Cochran said, "a beauty operator ceased to exist and an aviator was born."

Soon Jacqueline was the leading female pilot in the United States. In September of 1938, with just enough gas for another few minutes of flying, she won the transcontinental Bendix Race. This was a truly incredible feat: the former beautician flew the 2,042 miles from Los Angeles to Cleveland in an amazing 8 hours, 10 minutes, and 31 seconds. She was the first person to finish the course nonstop. More than once, she was awarded the women's Harmon Trophy, the highest honor given then to American women aviators. She also broke the women's altitude record and several speed records. "I might have been born in a hovel," Jacqueline said, "but I was determined to travel with the wind and the stars."

In 1943, during World War II, Jacqueline became the leader of the Women's Airforce Service Pilots, or WASPs. These pilots did jobs such as ferrying planes, training B-17 turret gunners, testing planes at repair depots, and teaching staff pilots at navigator schools. By the end of 1944, however, Congress unfairly refused to admit the WASPs into the military and ended the program. Despite her disappointment, Jacqueline continued to fly and set records until the 1970s, when health problems forced her to stop flying. She died in 1980.

Name ______________________________

Focus on Facts continued

Answer these questions about the passage on page 114.

1. What opinion about Jacqueline Cochran does the author give in the first paragraph?

____

____

2. The author includes several facts and one opinion in the second paragraph. Write them here.

Facts: ______________________________

____

____

____

Opinion: ______________________________

____

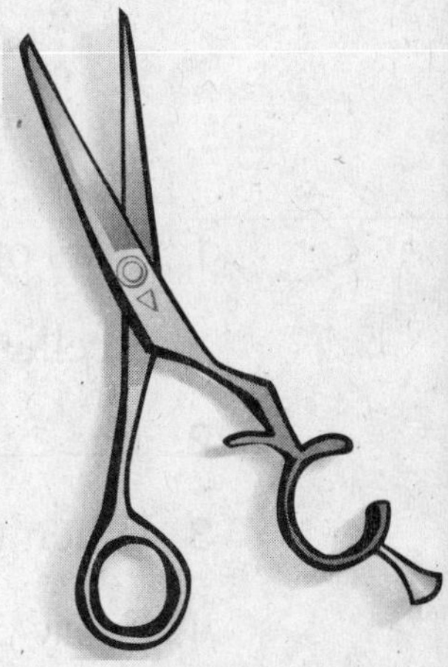

3. What opinion about Jacqueline's victory in the transcontinental Bendix Race does the author give in the third paragraph?

____

4. The author uses facts to support an opinion about Jacqueline's victory in the Bendix Race. What are they?

____

____

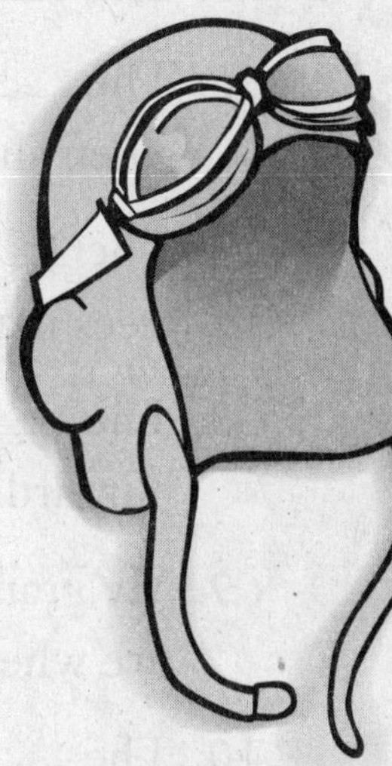

5. What opinion does the author give in the fourth paragraph?

____

____

6. Rewrite the following sentence so it states a fact and not an opinion: *Jacqueline Cochran was an amazing female aviator.*

____

____

Name ______________________________

Be a Searcher!

Amelia Earhart's plane has words on it. Circle each word that has a suffix meaning "someone who." Then use those words to complete the sentences.

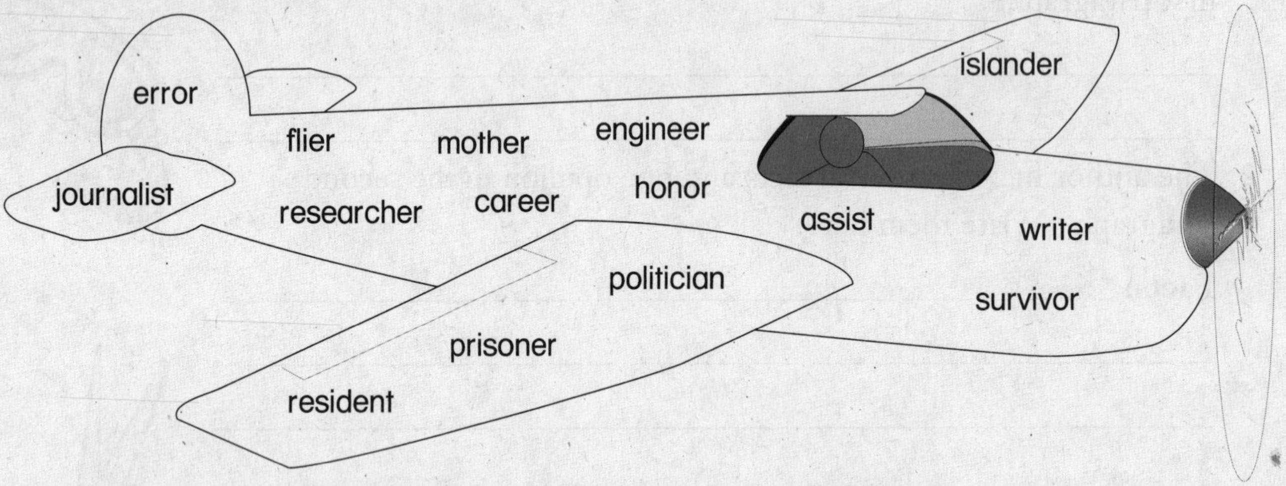

1. Years of training in how to handle a plane have made him an excellent ____________________.
2. The ____________________ thanked everyone who voted for her.
3. When the war was over, each ____________________ was set free.
4. Every ____________________ in the town had lived there at least five years.
5. The ____________________ took a boat to school every day.
6. The ____________________ had always liked to make up stories when she was a child.
7. The ____________________ is experimenting to find out how trees make oxygen.
8. The ____________________ reported on the record-breaking blizzard.
9. My grandfather was the only ____________________ of a house fire when he was young.
10. The ____________________ designed a new plan for the factory.

Name ______________________________

Vowel + /r/ Sounds

Remember the following spelling patterns for these vowel + /r/ sounds:

/ûr/	*ear, ur, ir*	**ear**th, **ur**ge, sk**ir**t
/ôr/	*or, our*	sc**or**n, m**our**n
/är/	*ar*	sn**ar**l
/îr/	*ier*	f**ier**ce

Write each Spelling Word under its vowel + /r/ sounds.

/ûr/ Sounds

____
____
____
____
____
____
____
____
____

/ôr/ Sounds

____
____
____
____
____

/är/ Sounds

____
____
____
____

/îr/ Sounds

____
____

Spelling Words

1. fierce
2. sword
3. court
4. snarl
5. thorn
6. earth
7. skirt
8. chart
9. urge
10. yarn
11. whirl
12. mourn
13. rehearse
14. curb
15. earnest
16. starch
17. purse
18. birch
19. pierce
20. scorn

Name ______________________________

Spelling Spree

Clues Write a Spelling Word for each clue.

1. You do this to prepare for a performance.
2. A judge presides there.
3. You step off this to cross a street.
4. A woman may wear one with a blouse.
5. A unfriendly dog may do this.
6. Some people ask the cleaner to add it to their laundry.
7. Its bark may be white and papery.
8. Kittens get tangled up in it.
9. You might find change in this.

1. ____________________
2. ____________________
3. ____________________
4. ____________________
5. ____________________
6. ____________________
7. ____________________
8. ____________________
9. ____________________

Word Search Write the Spelling Word that is hidden in each sentence.

Example: How is a <u>pear</u> like an apple? *pearl*

10. Everybody loves corn on the cob!
11. Did you hear that moaning sound?
12. The people at the pier celebrated the yacht's victory.
13. He gave me his word of honor.
14. The gardener will trim our new rosebushes.

10. ____________________
11. ____________________
12. ____________________
13. ____________________
14. ____________________

Spelling Words

1. fierce
2. sword
3. court
4. snarl
5. thorn
6. earth
7. skirt
8. chart
9. urge
10. yarn
11. whirl
12. mourn
13. rehearse
14. curb
15. earnest
16. starch
17. purse
18. birch
19. pierce
20. scorn

Name ______________________________

Proofreading and Writing

Proofreading Circle the six misspelled Spelling Words in this message. Then write each word correctly.

While we were flying toward Howland Island, we ran into some feirce winds. The plane began to wirl out of control. It came to earth on an island that Fred and I can't find on our cheart. Our supplies are running low, and the only plants on the island are thourn bushes that bear no fruit. We earge anyone who finds this message to contact the United States government. A rescue operation must be organized immediately. This is in ernest. It is not a prank!

1. ______________ 4. ______________

2. ______________ 5. ______________

3. ______________ 6. ______________

Spelling Words

1. fierce
2. sword
3. court
4. snarl
5. thorn
6. earth
7. skirt
8. chart
9. urge
10. yarn
11. whirl
12. mourn
13. rehearse
14. curb
15. earnest
16. starch
17. purse
18. birch
19. pierce
20. scorn

Write a Journal Entry Amelia was a unique individual who attempted a daring feat. Have you ever tried something that may have had some element of risk to it? Did anyone try to discourage you? Did you have doubts? How did you resolve the doubts? Use your own or someone else's experience to think about the idea of taking risks.

On a separate sheet of paper, write a journal entry about taking risks. Use Spelling Words from the list.

Name ______________________________

Stress on Syllables

Read each dictionary entry. Sound out the word several times, placing stress on a different syllable each time. Circle the choice with the correct stress.

1. **ap•proach** (ə **prōch′**) *v.* To come near or nearer in place or time.

   AP•proach   ap•PROACH

2. **a•vi•a•tion** (ā′ vē **ā′** shən) *n.* The art of operating and navigating aircraft.

   A•vi•a•tion   a•VI•a•tion   a•vi•A•tion   a•vi•a•TION

3. **cal•cu•late** (**kăl′** kyə lāt′) *v.* To find or determine an answer by using mathematics.

   CAL•cu•late   cal•CU•late   cal•cu•LATE

4. **con•ti•nent** (**kŏn′** tə nənt) *n.* One of the seven great land masses of the earth.

   CON•ti•nent   con•TI•nent   con•ti•NENT

5. **ex•haust•ed** (ĭg **zôst′** əd) *adj.* Completely worn-out; tired.

   EX•haust•ed   ex•HAUST•ed   ex•haust•ED

6. **fre•quen•cy** (**frē′** kwən sē) *n.* The number of complete cycles of a wave, such as a radio wave, that occur per second.

   FRE•quen•cy   fre•QUEN•cy   fre•quen•CY

7. **re•fu•el** (rē **fyo͞o′** əl) *v.* To provide with fuel again.

   RE•fu•el   re•FU•el   re•fu•EL

8. **re•verse** (rĭ **vûrs′**) *v.* To turn around to the opposite direction.

   RE•verse   re•VERSE

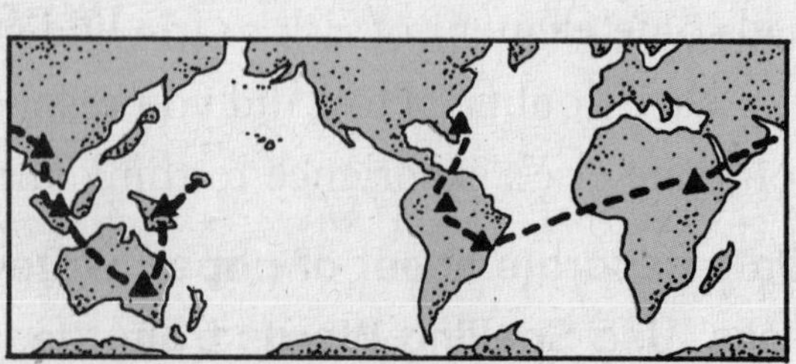

Name ______________________________

Amelia's Plane

Singular and Plural Possessive Nouns Possessive nouns show ownership or possession. To form the possessive of a singular noun, add an apostrophe and an *-s ('s)*. To form the possessive of a plural noun that ends in *-s*, add only an apostrophe ('). To form the possessive of a plural noun that does not end in *-s*, add an apostrophe and an *-s ('s)*.

singular noun: dog	**singular noun**: James
possessive: dog's	**possessive**: James's
plural noun: boys	**plural noun**: deer
possessive: boys'	**possessive**: deer's

Write the possessive form of each noun in parentheses.

1. the (plane) ______________ cockpit
2. the (women) ______________ plane

3. the (planes) ______________ hangar
4. the (man) ______________ binoculars

5. our (country) ______________ flag

Amelia Earhart: First Lady of Flight

Grammar Skill More Possessive Nouns

Name ______________________________

Amelia Earhart's Disappearance

More Possessive Nouns Remember how to form **possessive nouns**:

1. Add an apostrophe and an *-s ('s)* to a singular noun.
2. Add an apostrophe and an *-s ('s)* to a plural noun that does not end in *-s*.
3. Add an apostrophe (') to a plural noun that ends in *-s*.

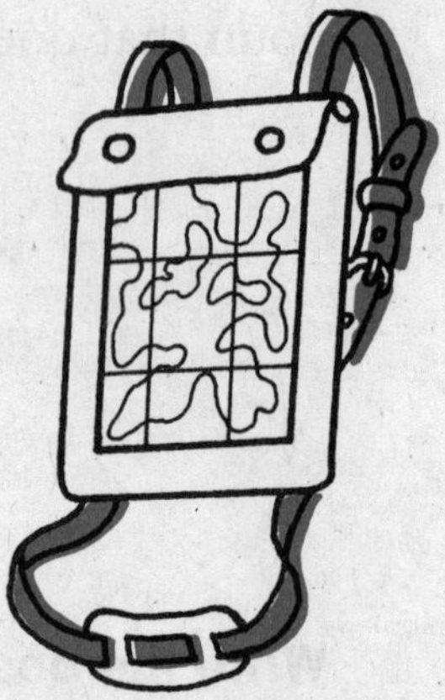

The following sentences use phrases that show possession or ownership. Revise each underlined phrase to use a possessive noun.

Example: Lynette visited the home of Amelia Earhart.
Lynette visited **Amelia Earhart's home**.

1. No one knows the fate of Amelia Earhart.

____

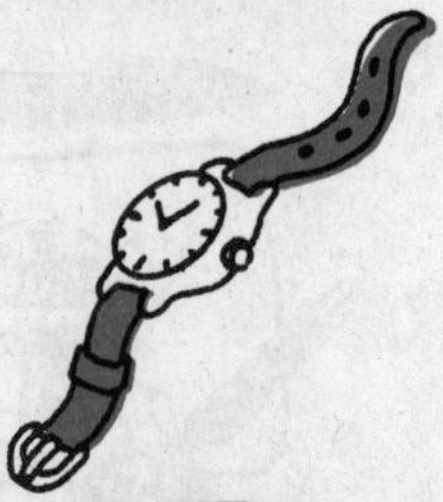

2. Her fate has aroused the interest of many people.

____

3. The theories of researchers are interesting to read.

____

4. The fascination of Ross with Earhart's disappearance has led him to read many books.

____

____

5. The planes of early pilots seem primitive today.

____

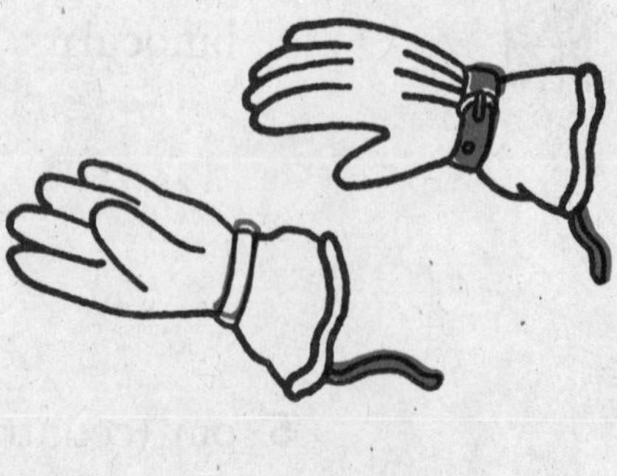

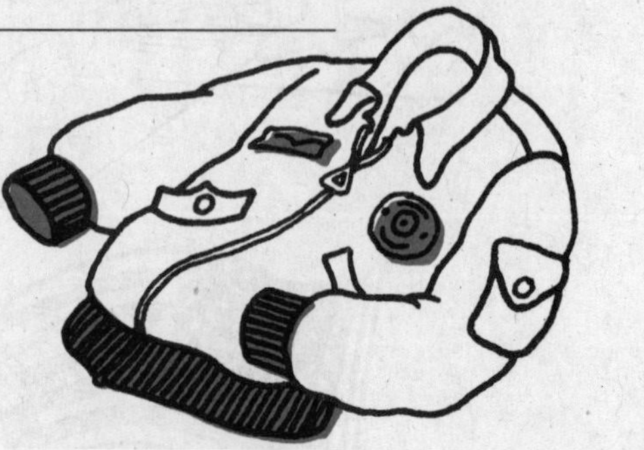

Name ___________________________

Write to My Friend

Using Apostrophes Writers use apostrophes in possessives and in contractions. If you leave an apostrophe out, you can confuse your reader. Likewise, if you use an apostrophe incorrectly, you can also confuse your reader. Look at how apostrophes change the meaning in the examples below.

We'll see you. Well see you. the dog's food the dogs' food

Proofread the following draft of a letter Lynette wrote to her friend in Kansas. Underline each error in the use of apostrophes in possessives and contractions. Then rewrite each underlined word correctly above the error.

Dear Carolyn,

Im so glad that I had the chance to visit you in Kansas last month. You ca'nt imagine how much I miss seeing you in school every day, but the town you now live in is beautiful. It is interesting that your town is also Amelia Earharts hometown. I enjoyed visiting her familys' house. Her story inspired me, and I havent stopped thinking about the mystery. What do you think really happened?

Your friend,
Lynnette

Name ________________________________

Writing a News Article

Amelia Earhart's disappearance over the Pacific Ocean during her 1937 flight around the world was front-page news. Imagine you are a reporter for the *World News and Recorder*. Use the chart below to gather facts and details for a *news article* about the disappearance of Earhart's plane or about another historic event. Answer these questions: Who was involved? What happened? When, where, and why did this event occur? How did it happen?

Who?	
What?	
When?	
Where?	
Why?	
How?	

Now use the details and facts you gathered to write your news article on a separate sheet of paper. Write a beginning that gives the facts, yet captures the reader's attention. Present the facts you recorded in the chart in the order of most to least important. Use quotations where possible to bring this news event to life, and include a headline that will grab your reader's attention.

Name ______________________________

Adding Details

A good reporter uses details to hold the interest of readers and satisfy their curiosity, to clearly explain what happened, and to make the people who were involved in the event come alive.

Read the following draft of a news article. Then rewrite it on the lines below, adding details from the list to improve it.

Aviator Mysteriously Vanishes

American aviator Amelia Earhart and her navigator mysteriously vanished in the skies on July 2, 1937. Earhart and Noonan were attempting a west-to-east flight. Their airplane, which departed from Lae, New Guinea, was headed northeast when it disappeared.

The last radio communication with Earhart occurred in the morning with William Galten, who serves aboard the United States Coast Guard cutter.

____

____

____

____

____

____

____

____

Details

Lockheed Electra	Frederick Noonan
over the Pacific Ocean	toward tiny Howland Island
Itasca	at 8:47 A.M.
around the world	Radioman Third Class

Name ______________________________

Revising Your Story

Reread your story. Put a checkmark in the box for each sentence that describes your paper. Use this page to help you revise.

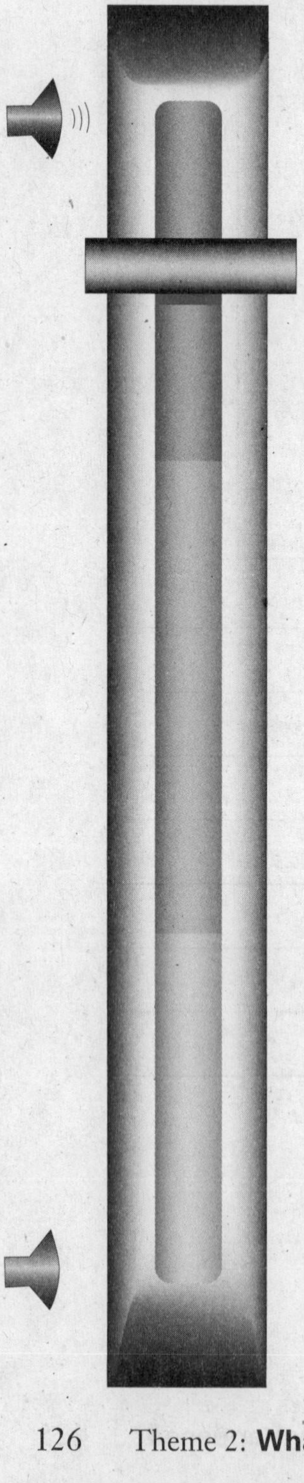

Loud and Clear!

☐ My story has a clear beginning, middle, and ending. It is focused on an interesting problem.

☐ Details and dialogue make characters seem real.

☐ I wrote in a way that gets my readers' attention.

☐ Many exact words create vivid pictures.

☐ Sentences flow smoothly. There are few mistakes.

Sounding Stronger

☐ My beginning, middle, or ending is unclear. The plot may not be focused on a problem.

☐ I need more details and dialogue for my characters.

☐ My writing won't always hold my reader's attention.

☐ My words are too vague. I could make them more exact.

☐ Some sentences are choppy. There are some mistakes.

Turn Up the Volume

☐ There is no beginning, middle, or ending. There is no problem.

☐ I didn't use any details. There is no dialogue.

☐ My writing sounds flat.

☐ I use the same word many times.

☐ Most sentences are choppy. There are many mistakes.

Name ______________________________________

Using Exact Nouns

Replace each underlined noun. In exercises 1–4, circle the letter of the noun that best completes each sentence. In exercises 5–8, write in a noun of your own choice.

1. A lion held a mouse in its hands and said, "Tell me why I should not eat you, little one."

   a. legs b. fingers c. paws d. jaws

2. "Because one day I may save you from a great situation," said the mouse.

   a. peril b. happiness c. accident d. elephants

3. The lion laughed. "How could a tiny mouse such as you ever help a great animal such as myself?" the lion asked.

   a. mammal b. beast c. critter d. freak

4. The lion let the mouse go and it escaped into the beyond.

   a. unknown b. trail c. cave d. jungle

5. Weeks later, the mouse heard a sound and found a lion caught in a net.

   ____

6. "Help me, little mouse," the lion cried. "I am in deep adversity."

   ____

7. With teeth as sharp as pins, the mouse ate through the net and freed the lion. "How can I ever repay you?" said the lion.

   ____

8. "You already have," said the mouse. "For I am the same mouse that you caught weeks ago. You let me make an exit then, so I helped you now."

   ____

Name ______________________________

Spelling Words

Look for familiar spelling patterns to help you remember how to spell the Spelling Words on this page. Think carefully about the parts that you find hard to spell in each word.

Write the missing letters in the Spelling Words below.

1. ton ___ ___ ___ t
2. ev ___ ___ ___ where
3. ev ___ ___ ___ body
4. ___ ___ other
5. bec ___ ___ ___ e
6. ___ ___ ole
7. p ___ ___ ple
8. c ___ ___ ___ ___ n
9. clo ___ ___ ___ s
10. h ___ ___ ___ ___ t
11. a ___ ___ ___ ys
12. r ___ ___ ___ t
13. m ___ ___ ___ t
14. re ___ ___ ___ y
15. ev ___ ___ ___ thing

Spelling Words

1. tonight
2. everywhere
3. everybody
4. another
5. because
6. whole
7. people
8. cousin
9. clothes
10. height
11. always
12. right
13. might
14. really
15. everything

Study List On a separate sheet of paper, write each Spelling Word. Check your spelling against the words on the list.

Name ______________________________

Spelling Spree

Syllable Scramble **Rearrange the syllables in each item to write a Spelling Word. There is one extra syllable in each item.**

1. ways al all
2. oth un an er
3. cause be coz
4. ry were eve where
5. nite night to
6. ple pe peo
7. ev thing ry eve
8. bo eve ry in dy

1. ____________
2. ____________
3. ____________
4. ____________
5. ____________
6. ____________
7. ____________
8. ____________

Spelling Words

1. tonight
2. everywhere
3. everybody
4. another
5. because
6. whole
7. people
8. cousin
9. clothes
10. height
11. always
12. right
13. might
14. really
15. everything

Find a Rhyme **Write a Spelling Word that rhymes with the underlined word and makes sense in the sentence.**

9. It looks like we _____ have to find another <u>site</u> for the building.
10. Somebody <u>stole</u> the _____ eight thousand dollars!
11. There's only a <u>slight</u> difference between your _____ and mine.
12. When she gets _____ mad, she gets a <u>steely</u> look in her eyes.
13. My brother really <u>loathes</u> buying new _____.
14. Turn the screw to the _____ until it gets really <u>tight</u>.
15. I'm going to pick up a <u>dozen</u> donuts for my _____.

9. ____________
10. ____________
11. ____________
12. ____________
13. ____________
14. ____________
15. ____________

Name ______________________________

Proofreading and Writing

Proofreading **Circle the five misspelled Spelling Words in this advertisement. Then write each word correctly.**

Read all about it!

You mite think you've heard the whole story behind last winter's plane crashes, but if you do, you're wrong. Do you want to know what realy happened? Then read the book that everyone everwhere is talking about! This book tells you evrything that you could want to know about why those flights went down. It just goes to show that you can't allways believe what you see on television!

Spelling Words

1. tonight
2. everywhere
3. everybody
4. another
5. because
6. whole
7. people
8. cousin
9. clothes
10. height
11. always
12. right
13. might
14. really
15. everything

1. ____________ 4. ____________

2. ____________ 5. ____________

3. ____________

Write a Tag-Team Mystery **Team up with a classmate. Then, taking turns writing sentences, write a mystery story. Use Spelling Words from the list.**

Name ______________________________

Fishing for the Right Word

Fill in each blank with a word from the box.

Vocabulary

- mainland
- suspicious
- common room
- sod
- hearth
- phases
- kayak
- sparkling
- village

1. If you are in a light, one-person boat traditionally used in the Arctic, you are in a ______________________.
2. If you watch the moon each night for a month, you will observe all its ______________________.
3. If you live in a very small settlement, you live in a ______________________.
4. If you had been alive hundreds of years ago, you might have cooked on a ______________________.
5. If you do not trust someone, you are ______________________ of that person.
6. If your roof is made of squares of soil held together with the roots of grasses, it is made of ______________________.
7. If you are on an island, you are not on the ______________________.
8. If you are looking at waves on which the sun is shining, you are seeing ______________________ waters.
9. If you are in the part of a traditional dwelling where family members gather, you are in the ______________________.

Name ______________________________

Inferences Chart

Question	Evidence from the Story	Own Knowledge	Inference
Pages 172–173 What does nature mean to the cousins and their culture?			
Pages 175–176 Why do you think Moon wants the most patient cousin for his wife?			
Page 176 What is the work Moon must do?			
Pages 178–179 Why are the star people lying facedown?			
Page 180 Why does Moon's wife cover her head with a blanket and say she has a pain on her face?			

Name ______________________________

Questioning the Answers

Write an answer for each question below.

1. When did the cousins fall in love with the Moon?

____

____

2. What did the cousins have to do in order to become the Moon's wife?

____

____

3. What happened to the cousin who opened her eye?

____

4. What did the Moon tell his wife not to do?

____

5. Who were the one-eyed people whom the Moon's wife met?

____

6. What did the Moon's wife find in the storeroom?

____

7. What happened to Moon's wife when she tried on one of his masks?

____

8. What job did the Moon give his wife?

____

____

Name ______________________________

Putting Clues Together

Read the passage. Then complete the activity on page 135.

Eos and Tithonus, A Greek Myth

It was still dark when Eos, the dawn, awoke. She rose from her pink pillows and pushed her yellow bedcover aside. Pale light glowed from her hair. Eos dipped her rosy fingers into a glass and sprinkled dewdrops over the world. Then she ran outside and threw open the palace gates. She shaded her eyes as four fiery stallions pulled a golden chariot with her brother Helios, the sun, through the gates into the early morning sky. After latching the gates, Eos yawned and strolled back into the palace.

From the bedroom she heard a tiny cough. Tithonus, her husband, must be awake. "Poor dear," Eos thought, hurrying to the bedside. She caught sight of herself in the mirror and couldn't help smiling. She didn't look a day over twenty, although she was far, far older than her husband.

Eos looked everywhere for Tithonus, but she couldn't find him. At last she spied him crouching in a corner, a shriveled, tiny man about the size of a grasshopper. In fact, his wheezing sounded a little like chirping. Eos sighed sadly. "He is quite old — almost 350," she thought. It seemed only yesterday that she had glimpsed him on Earth, the handsomest young man imaginable. She had begged Zeus to make him immortal so she could marry him. Zeus had done his best, but he'd warned her that something like this might happen.

After serving Tithonus a very small breakfast, she had an idea. Why not keep him in her little handkerchief basket? A basket might keep him safe, and it was certainly a better size for him than furniture in the palace. Tithonus did not object to his new home, and Eos set the basket on the windowsill so he could enjoy the sun. That night his sad chirping lulled her to sleep. When Eos peered into the basket next morning, she thought he looked greener than he did the day before.

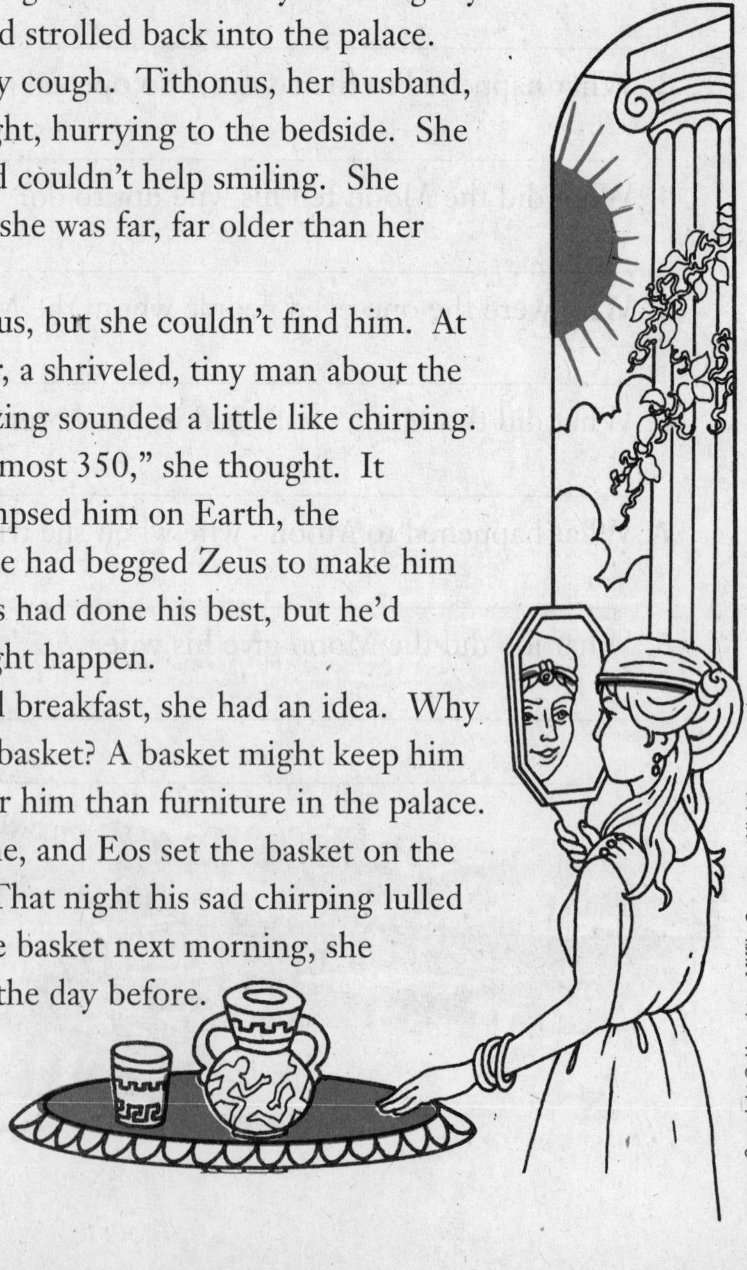

Name ______________________________

Putting Clues Together continued

Answer these questions about the story on page 134.

1. How does Eos feel about Tithonus?

____

2. What clues in the story tell you that Eos loves and pities her husband?

____

____

3. What has happened to Tithonus that has not happened to Eos?

____

____

4. What seems to be happening to Tithonus? How can you tell?

____

____

5. What do you think Tithonus might become? Why?

____

____

6. Myths and folktales often do more than entertain. What purpose do you think this story has? Circle one answer.

A. to teach a lesson about what is right

B. to explain how grasshoppers came to be

C. to explain the movement of the sun and moon

Name ______________________________

What's the Ending?

Read the letter. Circle the ten words with the endings -*s* or -*es*. Write each word in the first column, and then write the base word and the ending.

Dear cousin,

We have different lives now, and I won't see you again. But there are many possible husbands in the villages all around you. Do you still walk on the beaches in the evenings to glimpse the moon? If you look up, you will see me in the heavens. My husband and I share the cycles of the moon. He enjoys his work, and so do I. He carries the moon for the first half of each cycle, and I carry it for the second half. So, whenever the moon glimmers down on you, think of me.

Your loving cousin

	Word	Base word	Ending
1.			
2.			
3.			
4.			
5.			
6.			
7.			
8.			
9.			
10.			

Name ______________________________

Homophones

Words that sound alike but have different spellings and meanings are called **homophones**. When you use a homophone, be sure to spell the word that has the meaning you want.

vain	(vān)	unsuccessful, fruitless
vein	(vān)	a blood vessel

Write the homophone pairs among the Spelling Words.

Homophones

____________	____________
____________	____________
____________	____________
____________	____________
____________	____________
____________	____________
____________	____________
____________	____________
____________	____________
____________	____________

Spelling Words

1. fir
2. fur
3. scent
4. sent
5. scene
6. seen
7. vain
8. vein
9. principal
10. principle
11. manor
12. manner
13. who's
14. whose
15. tacks
16. tax
17. hangar
18. hanger
19. died
20. dyed

Name ______________________________

Spelling Spree

Homophone Riddles Write a pair of Spelling Words to complete each statement.

1–2. A hook to hang your coat on in an airport storage building is a _____ _____.
3–4. A dog might call the needles of a pine tree _____ _____.
5–6. The most important one in a set of rules or standards is the _____ _____.
7–8. A gift of perfume mailed to a friend is a _____ _____.

1. ____________________
2. ____________________
3. ____________________
4. ____________________
5. ____________________
6. ____________________
7. ____________________
8. ____________________

Spelling Words

1. fir
2. fur
3. scent
4. sent
5. scene
6. seen
7. vain
8. vein
9. principal
10. principle
11. manor
12. manner
13. who's
14. whose
15. tacks
16. tax
17. hangar
18. hanger
19. died
20. dyed

Familiar Phrases Write the Spelling Word that completes each phrase or sentence. Remember to capitalize the first word in a sentence.

9. as _____ as a peacock
10. a tie-_____ shirt
11. the _____ of the crime
12. not pushpins, but _____
13. draw blood from a _____
14. federal income _____
15. Knock, knock. _____ there?

9. ____________________
10. ____________________
11. ____________________
12. ____________________
13. ____________________
14. ____________________
15. ____________________

Name ____________________

Proofreading and Writing

Proofreading Circle the five misspelled Spelling Words in this e-mail message. Then write each word correctly.

To: The stars

SEND

From: Moon

Subject: My wife

Some of you may have sene my wife, who's been living up here for the past few months. She has been bored in our huge, empty mannor. Well, I have decided to let her share moon duties with me. She will carry the moon's light from full moon until it appears to have dide out. I have watched her practice, and she is doing well. She moves across the sky in just the right maner. My wife, who's days are now busy, is much happier and looks forward to meeting all of you.

1. ____________________
2. ____________________
3. ____________________
4. ____________________
5. ____________________

Spelling Words

1. fir
2. fur
3. scent
4. sent
5. scene
6. seen
7. vain
8. vein
9. principal
10. principle
11. manor
12. manner
13. who's
14. whose
15. tacks
16. tax
17. hangar
18. hanger
19. died
20. dyed

Write a Job Description Moon decided to give his wife half of his work to do, but suppose he had wanted to hire someone he didn't know. How would he have described the job in a Help Wanted ad?

On a separate sheet of paper, write a job description for Moon's work. Use Spelling Words from the list.

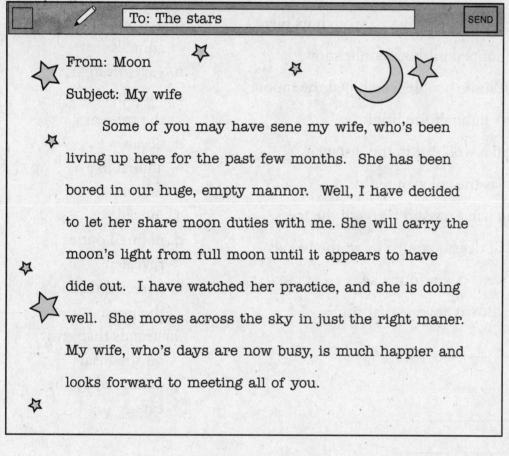

Name ______________________________

Match the Sounds

Match the correct definition to the boldface word. Then complete the homophone pairs below.

_____ 1. We can **see** the moon move through its phases.

_____ 2. The **hare** hopped in the moonlit snow.

_____ 3. In the **past** some people worshiped the moon.

_____ 4. The moon's light **shone** brightly.

_____ 5. They **heard** a wolf call in the distance.

_____ 6. Her **hair** was the color of night.

_____ 7. The raging wind **passed** through the trees.

_____ 8. The **herd** of deer bounded by in the woods.

_____ 9. The path went down to the **sea**.

_____ 10. Have you **shown** anyone that trail?

a. a group of wild animals
b. gave off light
c. the time before the present
d. ocean
e. animal like a rabbit
f. moved
g. pointed out or revealed
h. perceive through the eyes
i. strands that grow on the head
j. perceived by the ears

11. see ______________
12. hare ______________
13. past ______________
14. shone ______________
15. heard ______________

Name ____________________

We Collect Shells

Action Verbs and Direct Objects An **action verb** tells what the subject does. A **direct object** receives the action of the verb. To find the direct object in a sentence, first find the verb. Then ask who or what receives the action of the verb:

Jeff found a shell on the beach. The action verb is *found*. Jeff found *what* on the beach? He found a shell. *Shell* is the direct object.

The following sentence has a **compound direct object.**

Karen wore her jacket and scarf to the beach. The action verb is *wore*. Karen wore *what* to the beach? She wore her *jacket* and her *scarf*. The compound direct object is *jacket and scarf*.

Find the action verb and the direct object in each sentence below. Circle the verb and underline the direct object.

1. The older girls collect shells on the beach.
2. Grandfather builds a blazing fire.
3. Earlier, little Anna and Michael chased a flock of sandpipers.
4. Grandmother tells stories in the moonlight.
5. Father wraps Anna and Michael in a blanket.

Name ______________________________

Auxiliary Verbs Will Help Us

Main Verbs and Auxiliaries A **verb phrase** is made up of a main verb and an auxiliary. The **main verb** usually shows action. The **auxiliary** works with the main verb.

Common Auxiliary Verbs

am	were	do	has	must	might
is	be	does	had	will	would
are	being	did	can	shall	should
was	been	have	may	could	

What is the main verb in each sentence below? Is there an auxiliary verb? Fill in the chart below the sentences. If there is no auxiliary verb write *none*.

1. Peggy will tell us fascinating stories.
2. She has told two stories about her life.
3. Joan and Margaret have laughed harder than ever before.
4. Should Peggy repeat that story?
5. Peggy is a great storyteller!

	Main Verb	**Auxiliary Verb**
1.	______________	______________
2.	______________	______________
3.	______________	______________
4.	______________	______________
5.	______________	______________

Name ______________________________

Look at the Moon and Stars

Sentence Combining with Compound Direct Objects A good writer avoids writing too many short sentences, which can sound choppy. You can combine two sentences that have the same verb and different direct objects to make one sentence with a **compound direct object**.

Nora has **binoculars**. She has a **telescope** too.

Nora has **binoculars and a telescope.**

Here is the draft of an essay Nora is writing. Revise the draft by changing short, choppy sentences into sentences with compound direct objects. Write your version below.

Ancient people told stories about the moon. They told stories about the stars too. Today we have seen people on the moon. We have seen robots on Mars. Giant telescopes in the sky take pictures of Saturn. The telescopes take pictures of other planets too. Every night, I look at the moon through a telescope. I look at stars and planets too. Someday, I'll study Mars at an observatory. I'll also study Venus. I'll be a scientist. I'll be an astronaut. I'm shooting for the stars!

____

____

____

____

____

____

____

Name ___________________________________

Writing a Journal Entry

A **journal** is a notebook, diary, folder, or file in which you can record and save notes, lists, questions, ideas, thoughts, and feelings. For example, imagine that one of the two cousins in *The Girl Who Married the Moon* keeps a journal. She might write an entry to express her feelings about the Moon, to describe what happened when she received her chin tattoo, or to tell about such activities as weaving a basket from spruce roots or taking a sweat bath.

On the lines below, write your own journal entry for one day's events. Follow these guidelines:

- Write the date at the beginning. You may also want to note the location.
- Write in the first person, using the pronouns *I*, *me*, *my*, *mine*, *we*, and *our*.
- Describe the day's events or experiences.
- Include personal thoughts, feelings, reactions, questions, and ideas.
- Use sequence words when you narrate events.

____

____

____

____

____

____

____

____

____

____

When you finish your journal entry, you may want to share it with a friend or a classmate.

Name ______________________________

Using Exact Verbs

Good writers use exact verbs to bring their experiences to life. For example, exact verbs like *glow* or *sparkle* describe actions more precisely than does a common verb such as *shine*. When you write a journal entry, you can use exact verbs to create a more vivid picture of what happened.

Suppose this journal entry was written by the cousin who became the Moon's wife in *The Girl Who Married the Moon*. Read it and then rewrite it on the lines below, replacing the general verbs that have been underlined with more exact verbs from the list.

May 25, Moon's House

Today I felt incredibly bored, so I looked into Moon's storeroom and then went inside. What a surprise! Moon's storeroom is filled with sparkling pieces of light. I found all the moon phases except for the full moon. Now I know where my husband hides his phases.

The phases shined so temptingly! I took a piece of moon from a shelf and put it on my own face. Now the piece will not come off. What if Moon becomes angry?

____

____

____

____

____

____

____

____

Exact Verbs

conceals	peeked
placed	glittered
sneaked	discovered
plucked	crammed

Name ______________________________

Categorizing Vocabulary

Write each word from the box under the correct category.

Vocabulary

- theory
- erosion
- paleontologist
- extinct
- specimens
- geologists
- fossils
- hypotheses
- evidence
- excavation

two kinds of scientists

____

____

two kinds of artifacts

____

____

two names for beliefs based on facts and observations

____

____

a word for proof or support

____

two ways soil can be removed

____

____

a word for a vanished species of animals or plants

____

Now choose at least five words from the box. Use them to write a short paragraph about searching for the remains of ancient plants and animals.

____

____

____

____

____

____

____

Name ______________________________

Text Organization Chart

Organization: Main Ideas and Details

A Big Find of Small Dinosaurs

What did Dr. Ned Colbert find in 1947 at Ghost Ranch, New Mexico?

____

What question did Dr. Colbert's discovery make scientists ask themselves?

____

What Happened Here?

List two details about the dinosaur bones scientists found.

____

____

____

____

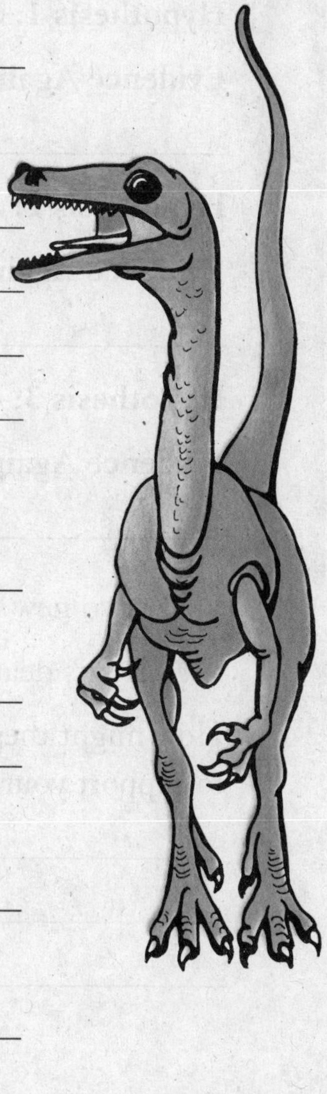

Organization: Hypothesis and Evidence

***Stuck in the Mud?* Hypothesis 1:**

____

Support *For* or *Against*:

____

____

***Volcanic Violence?* Hypothesis 2:**

____

Support *For* or *Against*:

____

____

____

Name ______________________________

What Happened to *Coelophysis*?

Scientists decided that the hypotheses below were *not* the best explanations for *Coelophysis*'s death. List the evidence *against* each one. Then answer the questions below.

Hypothesis Notes: *Why Coelophysis might have died*
Hypothesis 1: *Stuck in mud*
Evidence Against: ______________________________
____

Hypothesis 2: *Volcanic eruption*
Evidence Against: ______________________________
____

Hypothesis 3: *Asteroid fallout caused starvation*
Evidence Against: ______________________________
____

What two new hypotheses did scientists decide best explain *Coelophysis*'s death? ____________________ and ____________________

How might these two hypotheses have worked together? Give evidence to support your explanation.
____
____
____

Name ___________________________________

Taking Text Apart

Read the article. Then answer the questions on page 150.

Trapped in Amber

A clear golden lump sells for $27,000 at an auction. This lump of *amber*, as the material is called, started out as sap from a tree. What makes it so valuable now? Look closely — inside the amber is a small thirty-million-year-old lizard.

What Is Amber?

Amber is hardened sap from ancient trees. Over millions of years the sap has changed into a rock-hard material. Because it is beautiful and lasts many years, amber is often used in jewelry. Some amber pieces give scientists a rare opportunity to study prehistoric *inclusions* such as leaves, insects, and reptiles preserved in the once-sticky sap.

How Does Amber Form?

Picture this process. Long ago (perhaps as long ago as the age of dinosaurs), sap oozes from a tree. It hardens on the tree trunk and is covered by more sap. After many years, the tree dies and decays. It is swept into a stream and eventually ends up under the sea or beneath layers of rock. If the sap had been left out in the air, it would have rotted. Because the sap is not exposed to oxygen, however, its molecules change, forming stronger and stronger bonds. Eventually, all its oils evaporate, and it becomes hard and shiny, a beautiful golden brown. It becomes amber.

How Is Something Trapped in Amber?

It is possible today to see plants, insects, and even small reptiles from long ago preserved in amber. How did they get there? Here is one way this might have happened: an unlucky insect lands on a tree trunk that is sticky with sap. It gets stuck. More sap flows down the tree, entirely covering the bug. Over the centuries the sap slowly turns to amber. The insect dries out but otherwise stays perfectly preserved.

Name ______________________________

Taking Text Apart continued

Answer these questions about the passage on page 149.

1. How many sections does the article have? (Don't count the introductory paragraph.)

   ____

2. What feature of the text helps you identify the different sections?

   ____

3. Reread the section under the heading *What Is Amber?* Is it organized by main idea and details, or by sequence of events?

   ____

4. Reread the section under the heading *How Does Amber Form?* Is this section organized by main idea and details, or by sequence?

   ____

5. What sequence words or phrases can you find in the second section? Write them here.

   ____

Name ______________________________

Sorting Out Suffixes

Read this field diary page. Underline each word with the suffix *-al, -ive,* or *-ous.*

Beginning today, we will use our best investigative methods to figure out why so many dinosaurs died here. The area is one massive burial ground. There are so many skeletons, it looks almost comical, as though the dinosaurs were gathering to watch a famous celebrity when they died. We know that this animal was carnivorous because of the bones of other animals in the skeletons' bellies. Our theories may be experimental, but only if we are creative and inventive can we solve the mystery. Really, it is marvelous work.

Now write the words you underlined. Use the paragraph above to help you find the meaning of each word.

1. ______________________________
2. ______________________________
3. ______________________________
4. ______________________________
5. ______________________________
6. ______________________________
7. ______________________________
8. ______________________________
9. ______________________________
10. ______________________________

Name ______________________________

Final /ər/, /ən/, and /əl/

The **schwa sound,** shown as /ə/, is a weak vowel sound often found in an unstressed syllable. Remember the following spelling patterns for the /ə/ sound:

final /ər/	*er, or, ar*	messeng**er**, direct**or**, simil**ar**
final /n/ or /ən/	*on, en*	weap**on**, fright**en**
final /l/ or /əl/	*le, el, al*	strugg**le**, chann**el**, ment**al**

► The spelling of the final /ər/ sound in *acre* differs from the usual patterns. The final /ər/ sound in *acre* is spelled *re*.

Write each Spelling Word under its final sound.

Final /ər/ Sound

____
____
____
____
____
____
____
____
____
____

Final /n/ or /ən/ Sound

____
____
____
____

Final /l/ or /əl/ Sound

____
____
____
____
____
____

Spelling Words

1. struggle
2. director
3. weapon
4. similar
5. mental
6. frighten
7. channel
8. messenger
9. familiar
10. acre*
11. error
12. gallon
13. rural
14. calendar
15. elevator
16. stumble
17. youngster
18. kitchen
19. passenger
20. quarrel

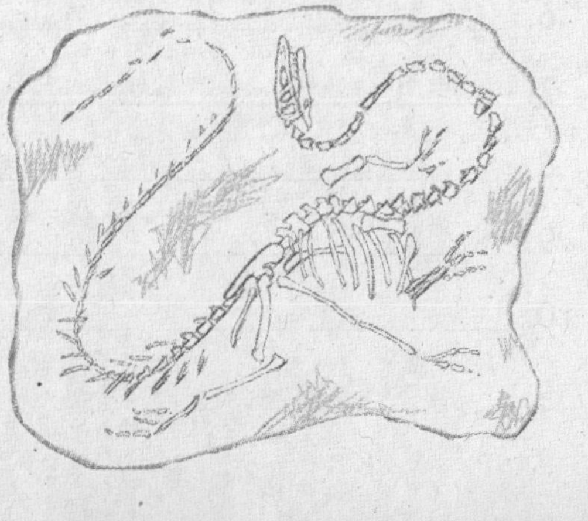

Name ______________________

Spelling Spree

Match Game **Match each word beginning below to an ending to form a Spelling Word. Then write each word correctly.**

Word Beginnings	Word Endings
1. ac	on
2. quarr	er
3. weap	le
4. elevat	en
5. stumb	al
6. ment	re
7. messeng	or
8. kitch	el

1. ______________ 5. ______________
2. ______________ 6. ______________
3. ______________ 7. ______________
4. ______________ 8. ______________

Syllable Spot **Write the Spelling Word that includes one of the syllables in each word below.**

Example: format *matter*

9. frightfully ______________
10. gallery ______________
11. passage ______________
12. correction ______________
13. tunnel ______________
14. calculate ______________
15. fanatic ______________

Spelling Words

1. struggle
2. director
3. weapon
4. similar
5. mental
6. frighten
7. channel
8. messenger
9. familiar
10. acre*
11. error
12. gallon
13. rural
14. calendar
15. elevator
16. stumble
17. youngster
18. kitchen
19. passenger
20. quarrel

Name ______________________________

Proofreading and Writing

Proofreading Circle the five misspelled Spelling Words in this journal entry. Then write each word correctly.

July 25

After weeks in this rurel area searching for dinosaur skeletons, I have finally had some success. Today, I found several skeletons similiar to *Coelophysis*. However, unless I made an errer in my measurements, these are larger and have a sturdier bone structure. The smallest, probably a yongster, is the most curious. It seems to have died in some sort of strugle. The rest of the skeletons are spread over an acre of land, and I have not had time to analyze them in detail. It looks like my work is cut out for me.

1. ______________
2. ______________
3. ______________
4. ______________
5. ______________

Spelling Words

1. struggle
2. director
3. weapon
4. similar
5. mental
6. frighten
7. channel
8. messenger
9. familiar
10. acre*
11. error
12. gallon
13. rural
14. calendar
15. elevator
16. stumble
17. youngster
18. kitchen
19. passenger
20. quarrel

Write an Explanation What do you think about the answer put forward in the selection for why so many dinosaur skeletons have been found at Ghost Ranch? Do you think the conclusions match the evidence? What about the possibility of new evidence suggesting another explanation?

On a separate piece of paper, write a short description of how you think the dinosaur skeletons wound up at Ghost Ranch. Use Spelling Words from the list.

Dinosaur Ghosts

Vocabulary Skill Dictionary: Spelling Table/Pronunciation Key

Name ______________________________

Discovering the Key

Use the spelling table/pronunciation key below to figure out how to pronounce each underlined vowel sound. Find a word in the vocabulary box with a similar vowel sound, and write that word after the sentence.

Spellings	Sample Words
a, ai, ei, ey	made, plait, vein, they
e, ee, ie, y	these, fleet, chief, bumpy
o, oe, ou, ow	fold, toe, boulder, slow
o, u, ou, oo	stomach, cut, rough, flood

Vocabulary

blow
late
nut
reel
sail
ton

1. Shoulder bones were found among the fossils.

____

2. The scientists found dozens of skeletons of the little dinosaur.

____

3. Each specimen was carefully weighed and recorded.

____

4. The dinosaurs hunted for prey along rivers and lakes.

____

5. Red blood cells were made in the marrow cavity.

____

6. These dinosaurs had no armor to shield themselves from predators.

____

Name ______________________________

Dinosaurs Eat . . .

Transitive and Intransitive Verbs A **transitive verb** is an action verb with a **direct object**, which receives the action. An **intransitive verb** has no direct object. See the examples below.

Verb	Transitive	Intransitive
read	I **read** the book.	I **read** quickly.
sit	(none)	They **sit** on the bus.
visit	He **visits** the ranch.	He **visits** often.

Underline the verb or verb phrase in each sentence below. Then write *transitive* or *intransitive* after the sentence.

1. Maurice saw a movie about dinosaurs. ______________________
2. I researched prehistoric times. ______________________
3. My friend went to the La Brea Tar Pits. ______________________
4. Some dinosaurs ate meat. ______________________
5. We will see dinosaur bones at the museum. ______________________
6. Dinosaurs lived during the Mesozoic era. ______________________
7. Some dinosaurs hunted other animals. ______________________
8. Still other dinosaurs munched plants. ______________________
9. Birds may have evolved from dinosaurs. ______________________
10. Not all dinosaurs grew to become giants. ______________________

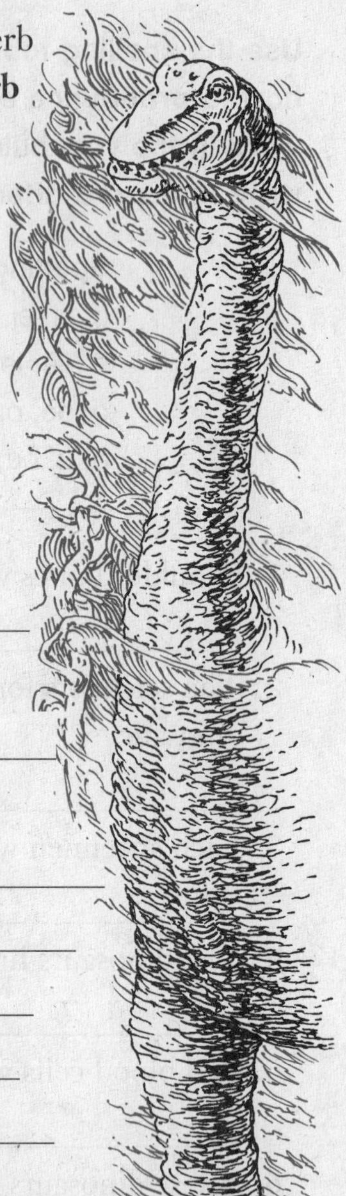

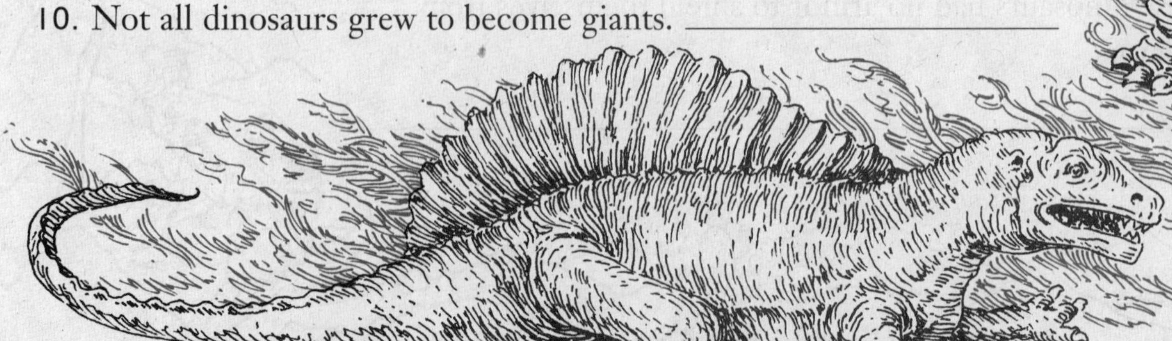

Name ______________________________

Dinosaurs Are Extinct

Being Verbs and Linking Verbs A **being verb** shows a state of being, not action. A **being verb** is called a **linking verb** when it links the subject to a predicate noun or a predicate adjective. A **predicate noun** identifies or renames the subject. A **predicate adjective** describes the subject.

Common Being and Linking Verbs				
am	was	be	become	feel
is	were	being	look	taste
are	seem	been	appear	smell

Underline the linking verb in each sentence below. After each sentence, write whether the verb links to a predicate noun or predicate adjective.

Example: Some dinosaurs were giants. predicate noun

1. The paleontologist seems excited by that stone. ____________
2. That stone is a fossil of a dinosaur. ____________
3. The work of a paleontologist looks interesting to me. ____________
4. Fossils of ferns are common here. ____________
5. A paleontologist is a scientist. ____________

Name ______________________________________

Dinosaurs Was/Were . . .

Using Forms of the Verb *be* A good writer uses the correct form of the verb *be*, especially when writing sentences with linking verbs. Study the present and past tense forms of the verb *be* in the chart below.

	Present Tense	Past Tense
Singular	I am	I was
	You are	You were
	She/he/it is	She/he/it was
Plural	We are	We were
	You are	You were
	They are	They were

Below is the beginning of a report written by a student who found a fossil. Write the correct form of the verb *be* above any incorrect verbs.

Example: I were tired. (was)

My brother and I is interested in dinosaurs. Yesterday, we was at the creek looking for fossils. My brother showed me a good place to look. It were a place with a lot of slate. I didn't think we'd find anything because fossils is hard to find. I are happy to tell you that I was wrong. I found a fossil impression of a tiny snail in a piece of slate.

Name ______________________________

Writing a Business Letter

When Ned Colbert in *Dinosaur Ghosts* began to study *Coelophysis* skeletons in 1947, he probably wrote business letters to ask paleontologists at other museums and universities around the United States for help. You write a **business letter** to request or persuade someone to do something, to apply for a job, to order a product from ads or catalogs, to ask for information, to complain about a product or service, or to express an opinion to a newspaper, radio, or TV station.

Use this page to plan and organize a business letter in which you write to either a company or a government agency requesting information. Follow these steps:

1. Write a **heading** (your own address and the date) in the upper right corner.
2. Write the **inside address** (the address of the person or business you are writing to) at the left margin.
3. Write a **greeting** *(Dear Sir or Madam:* or *Dear [business name]:)* at the left margin below the inside address.
4. Write the **body** of your letter below the greeting. Be brief and direct, but present all of the necessary details. If you state an opinion, support it with details. Make sure to use a formal and polite tone.
5. Write a formal **closing** such as *Sincerely*, *Cordially*, or *Yours truly* in the lower right corner.
6. Sign your full name under the closing. Then print or type your name below your **signature**.

When you finish your business letter, copy it onto a clean sheet of paper. Then share it with a classmate.

Name ______________________________

Using the Right Tone

The attitude that a writer has toward a subject is called the **tone**. A writer's choice of words and details conveys his or her tone. When you write a business letter, you want to create a good impression by using the right tone. Here are some tips to follow: Use polite language. Use a more formal tone than you would use in a friendly letter. Use correct grammar, complete sentences, and well-formed paragraphs. Avoid the use of slang. Do not include personal information.

Read the following business letter from a college student to Ned Colbert. Fill in the chart below with examples of language and details that are *not* businesslike.

Dear Ned,

Wow! I seen the cool photographs of your project in Life magazine. I do not have anything better to do, so I am interested in coming to New Mexico this summer to help with the Coelophysis excavation at Ghost Ranch. Would you tell me how to join your field crew?

I am fascinated by the Ghost Ranch skeletons. Since I will be studying history and geology next semester, this job would give me some excellent firsthand knowledge. I am a hard worker. Ask anyone at the Ribs Palace on Route 120 where I used to work. Keep in touch.

Sincerely,
Dennis Sauer

Slang	
Impolite Language	
Informal Tone	
Personal Information	
Incorrect Grammar	

Name ______________________________

Key Vocabulary

Use the words in the box to complete the sentences below.

1. A large group of people gathered together is a ______________________.
2. One type of lightweight volcanic rock is called ______________________.
3. Someone who has been pushed or elbowed has been ______________________.
4. A shaking or vibrating motion is a ______________________.
5. Broken pieces of rock and stone are ______________________.
6. A servant in charge of a household is a ______________________.

Vocabulary

steward
jostled
tremor
pumice
throng
rubble

Use four of the words from the sentences above to write a short paragraph describing what it might be like to experience a natural disaster.

____

____

____

____

Name ______________________________

Infer and Compare

As you read each selection, use the chart below to write down details about Eros and Giuseppe Fiorelli. Then use your own experience to make an inference about each person.

	Eros	Giuseppe Fiorelli
Details		
I know that		
Inference		

Name ______________________________

Connecting and Comparing

Think about the setting of *Pompeii.* How has the author helped you put yourself in that time and place? Fill out the chart with information about the setting of *Pompeii.* Then choose another selection in this theme in which the setting is important, and complete the chart.

	Selection Title: ***Pompeii***	**Selection Title:** ______________
The Setting		
Descriptive Language About the Setting		
Why the Setting Is Important		

Name ______________________________

Excavation Word Match-up

Match the words with their definitions.

1. spewed	a huge group of rocks moving down a hill
2. avalanche	to send out violently
3. glimpse	a quick look at something

Use each of the words below in a sentence.

4. spewed: ______________________________

5. avalanche: ______________________________

6. glimpse: ______________________________

Name ______________________________

Test Practice

Use the three steps you've learned to choose the best answer to complete these sentences about *Epilogue*. Fill in the circle for the best answer in the answer row at the bottom of the page.

1. The author's main purpose for writing *Epilogue* was to ______________.

- **A** provide more information about Eros
- **B** tell what scientists learned about the eruption
- **C** explain the warning signs of a volcano eruption
- **D** compare two ways of excavating ancient cities

2. Giuseppe Fiorelli improved the way Pompeii was being excavated by ______________.

- **F** looking for valuable artifacts
- **G** punishing sloppy archeologists
- **H** using an organized system for the excavation
- **J** destroying artifacts that were not important

3. One reason that people returned to Pompeii just after the eruption was to ______________.

- **A** begin construction of new buildings
- **B** seek shelter from the extreme heat
- **C** find food to eat
- **D** search for valuables

4. **Connecting/Comparing** The descriptions of the eruption in *Pompeii* and *Epilogue* are based partly on ______________.

- **F** information from Pliny's uncle
- **G** the letters of Pliny
- **H** a written account by Eros
- **J** writings found in Pompeii

ANSWER ROWS
1 Ⓐ Ⓑ Ⓒ Ⓓ   3 Ⓐ Ⓑ Ⓒ Ⓓ
2 Ⓕ Ⓖ Ⓗ Ⓙ   4 Ⓕ Ⓖ Ⓗ Ⓙ

Continue on page 166.

Name ______________________________

Test Practice continued

5. Objects that have been buried for centuries in volcanic pumice and ash are most likely ____________.
   - **A** well preserved
   - **B** highly valuable
   - **C** completely crushed
   - **D** extremely hot

6. In the late 1700s, statues, coins, and other valuable items were uncovered by ____________.
   - **F** Giuseppe Fiorelli
   - **G** Amedeo Maiuri
   - **H** treasure hunters
   - **J** survivors of the eruption

7. Some of the objects found in the House of the Menander show that ____________.
   - **A** the house was owned by Eros
   - **B** some people of Pompeii farmed
   - **C** the house had just been built
   - **D** houses in Pompeii were small

8. **Connecting/Comparing** The scientists in both *Epilogue* and *Dinosaur Ghosts* are working to ____________.
   - **F** understand events that occurred long ago
   - **G** prove that life is less dangerous today than long ago
   - **H** gain wealth and fame
   - **J** prevent a new disaster

ANSWER ROWS 5 Ⓐ Ⓑ Ⓒ Ⓓ 7 Ⓐ Ⓑ Ⓒ Ⓓ
6 Ⓕ Ⓖ Ⓗ Ⓙ 8 Ⓕ Ⓖ Ⓗ Ⓙ

Name ______________________

Facts or Opinions?

Read each sentence. Label each Fact or Opinion. If an opinion is supported by a fact, write the fact on the line below it.

1. Perhaps most of the people in Pompeii first thought that the eruption of Vesuvius was another earthquake.

____

2. The people who remained in Pompeii died from the extreme heat or were suffocated by hot ash.

____

3. Pompeii was buried under a thick blanket of pumice and ash.

____

4. Heat from the eruption of Vesuvius probably caused Pliny's uncle to die.

____

5. Amedeo Maiuri discovered the house of Menander between 1927 and 1932.

____

6. We believe that the house of Menander was one of the finest in Pompeii.

____

7. I think that putting Giuseppe Fiorelli in charge of the excavation of Pompeii was a good decision.

____

____

8. The buildings and objects uncovered in Pompeii allow us to see what life was like long ago.

____

Monitoring
Student Progress

Comprehension Skill
Text Organization

Name ______________________________

Looking Closely at Text

Read the article. Then answer the questions.

Volcanoes, Volcanoes, Volcanoes

Volcanoes have formed in various places, but most are found along the edges of the Earth's plates. Volcanoes have many different shapes and sizes. One classification system separates them into three main types, based on their shape and the materials from which they are formed: cinder cones, shield volcanoes, and composite volcanoes.

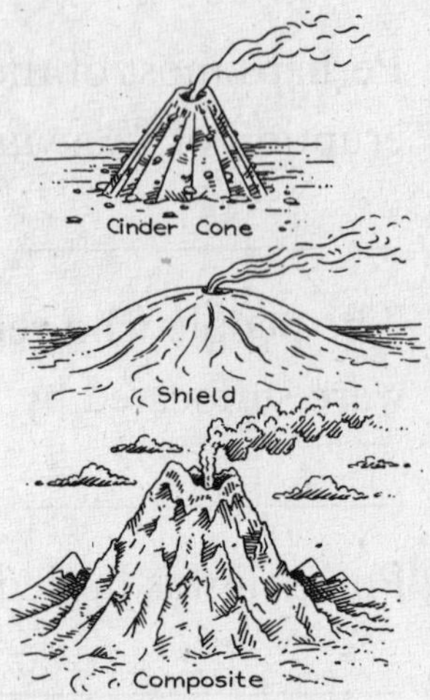

Cinder Cone Volcanoes

These volcanoes are formed when rock fragments, made of sticky magma, erupt through an opening or vent. When the fragments or cinders fall back to the ground around the vent, they form a mountain shaped like a cone.

Shield Volcanoes

These volcanoes are formed when lava flows from a vent. The lava spreads out and slowly builds up to form a low, dome-shaped mountain.

Composite Volcanoes

These volcanoes are formed when both rock fragments and lava flow from a vent. The materials pile up to form a tall mountain in the shape of a cone. Mount Vesuvius is one example of this type of volcano.

1. What are the different sections of this article about? ______________________________
2. What text feature helped you answer the first question? ______________
3. What text feature helps you know what the different types of volcanoes look like? ______________
4. How do you know which type of volcano is represented by each illustration? ______________
5. How are the sections of this article organized—by main ideas and details, by sequence of events, or by cause and effect? ______________

Name ______________________________

Sentences with Suffixes

Read the sentences. Underline each word with the suffix *-ous, -ive,* or *-al.*

1. The eruption of Mount Vesuvius is a famous event.
2. The force of the eruption was so explosive that it destroyed many buildings.
3. The ash cloud was disruptive to life even many miles away from the volcano.
4. Gases from the volcano were hazardous to all people and animals.
5. Despite the destruction, the eruption was a natural event.
6. Archaeologists found many cultural artifacts buried in the rubble.

Now write the words you underlined along with their meanings. Use the meanings of the base word and suffix along with sentence context to help you.

1. ______________________________
2. ______________________________
3. ______________________________
4. ______________________________
5. ______________________________
6. ______________________________

Name ______________________________

Pronunciation Practice

Read each sentence below. Use the pronunciation key to figure out how to pronounce each underlined vowel sound. Then list a sample word that uses the same spelling for that vowel sound.

ŭ	pat, laugh	ŏ	horrible, pot
ā	ape, aid, pay	ō	go, row, toe, though
ĕ	pet, pleasure, wear	ô	all, caught, paw
ē	be, bee, easy, piano		

1. The light streamed through the window. ______________________
2. The man saw the leather purse. ______________________
3. He lay on a narrow bed. ______________________
4. The man's daughter was found nearby. ______________________
5. A blanket of ash covered the walls. ______________________
6. Escape was not possible. ______________________
7. She could not see the dog below her feet. ______________________
8. We took shelter from the rain of ash. ______________________

Name ______________________________

Spelling Review

Write Spelling Words from the list to answer the questions.

1–24. Which twenty-four words contain the /ûr/, /ôr/, /är/, or /îr/ sounds, or have the final /ər/, /ən/, or /əl/ sounds?

1. ____________ 13. ____________
2. ____________ 14. ____________
3. ____________ 15. ____________
4. ____________ 16. ____________
5. ____________ 17. ____________
6. ____________ 18. ____________
7. ____________ 19. ____________
8. ____________ 20. ____________
9. ____________ 21 ____________
10. ____________ 22. ____________
11. ____________ 23. ____________
12. ____________ 24. ____________

25–30. Which six one-syllable words are homophones?

25. ____________ 28. ____________
26. ____________ 29. ____________
27. ____________ 30. ____________

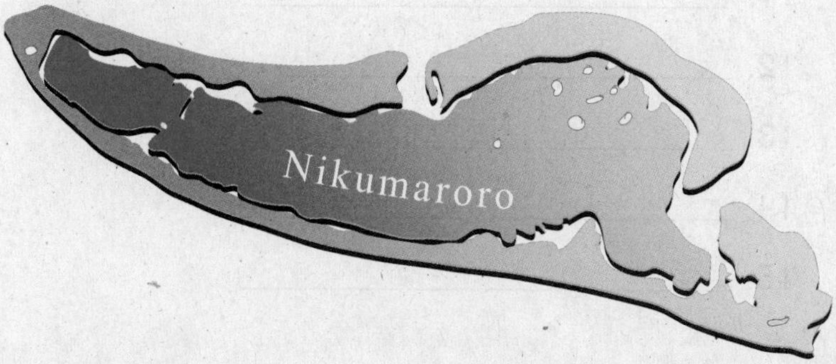

Spelling Words

1. channel
2. familiar
3. hanger
4. who's
5. chart
6. calendar
7. rehearse
8. starch
9. purse
10. whose
11. hangar
12. curb
13. mourn
14. director
15. frighten
16. manor
17. thorn
18. vain
19. messenger
20. pierce
21. struggle
22. sent
23. vein
24. manner
25. sword
26. similar
27. scent
28. whirl
29. gallon
30. rural

Name ______________________________

Spelling Spree

Syllable Scramble **Rearrange the syllables in each item to write a Spelling Word. There is one extra syllable in each item.**

Example: er for sid con *consider*

1. sen ger mes ize ____________
2. en cal men dar ____________
3. ger iar mil fa ____________
4. hearse in re ____________
5. rec na tor di ____________

Word Maze **Begin at the arrow and follow the Word Maze to find ten Spelling Words. Write the words in the order you find them.**

Start → r o s s t a r c h q p u r s e y u v a i n i t

y t d s c e n t l a v e i n g o v

e f r i g h t e n o p e c u r b i f g a l l o n

p y p o m a n n e r

q u p o m o u r n w a t

6. ____________
7. ____________
8. ____________
9. ____________
10. ____________
11. ____________
12. ____________
13. ____________
14. ____________
15. ____________

Spelling Words

1. familiar
2. calendar
3. mourn
4. frighten
5. gallon
6. rehearse
7. starch
8. purse
9. director
10. vain
11. messenger
12. scent
13. curb
14. vein
15. manner

Name ______________________________

Proofreading and Writing

Proofreading **Circle the six misspelled Spelling Words in this detective's journal. Then write each word correctly.**

The case of Mrs. VanCash's jewels has put me into a whurl. At first I didn't know how to chaurt a course. It's been a real struggel for me, Sherlock McGillicuddy, to find the truth. The mystery was truly a thorne in my side! When the maid swore the jewels were hers, I wondered whos they really were. Then I solved the mystery! The maid was telling the truth. Her jewels were simalar to the stolen ones, but hers were fakes.

1. ____________________ 4. ____________________
2. ____________________ 5. ____________________
3. ____________________ 6. ____________________

Spelling Words

1. channel
2. hanger
3. who's
4. chart
5. whose
6. hangar
7. thorn
8. pierce
9. struggle
10. sword
11. similar
12. sent
13. whirl
14. manor
15. rural

Reporting the Facts **Write the Spelling Words that best complete this television news report.**

An ancient, long-bladed 7. ______________ has been found in a 8. ______________ area outside town. The weapon was found in an old airplane 9. ______________. A worker picked it up, thinking it was a coat 10. ______________. Experts believe this may be the blade used centuries ago to 11. ______________ a stone near the 12. ______________ house of Sir Percy. The blade will be 13. ______________ to a lab for testing. Now the question is, 14. ______________ going to claim this treasure? Stay tuned to this 15. ______________!

Write a Plot Outline **On a separate sheet of paper, write a plot outline for a story about an unsolved mystery.**

Name ______________________________

Working with Possessive Nouns

Draw a line under each possessive noun. Write whether it is a singular possessive noun or a plural possessive noun.

1. An earthquake's rumble is terrifying.
   ____
2. The tremors can frazzle residents' nerves.
   ____
3. A volcano's eruption is an awesome event.
   ____
4. Children's parents rush them to safe places.
   ____
5. Even a minor eruption's effects can cause devastation.
   ____

Write the possessive form of each noun in parentheses.

6. the (tree) ______________ branches
7. the (lava) ______________ heat
8. the (rescuers) ______________ equipment
9. the (geese) ______________ cries
10. the (reporters) ______________ descriptions

Name ______________________________

Finding Action Verbs and Direct Objects

Find the action verb and the direct object in each sentence below. Circle the verb and underline the direct object or direct objects. Not every sentence has a direct object.

1. Guiseppe Fiorelli led the first organized excavation of Pompeii.
2. This archaeologist developed a sensible plan.
3. He made accurate maps and detailed lists.
4. Workers restored buildings under his guidance.
5. Looting of art treasures diminished significantly.
6. Another archaeologist made a wonderful discovery in Pompeii in the late 1920s.
7. He uncovered an ancient mansion.
8. Diggers found two chests with gold and silver treasures.
9. The workers discovered several bodies among the ruins there.
10. Many unfortunate people perished in the terrible eruption.

Name ______________________________

Playing It Up

Use the words in the box to complete the description of a play below.

Vocabulary

- actors
- audience
- cast
- character
- comedy
- dialogue
- drama
- perform
- stage directions
- tragedy

I saw a wonderful play last night. It was a very funny ______________ about two twin brothers on a Kansas farm who always get mistaken for each other. My favorite ______________ in the play was their mother, who like everyone else in the story couldn't tell her sons apart!

All the ______________ in the ______________ did a good job making their words and actions believable. I'll bet they were happy to ______________ in such an amusing play. I think the playwright did an excellent job with the ______________ because everyone in the ______________ laughed at all the jokes. From the way the actors moved and spoke, the ______________ seemed pretty funny also.

There was a lot of ______________ and emotion in the play as well as laughs, although no one would ever mistake it for a ______________. The show is still playing for one more week, so I suggest you and your family go see it. To miss such a fun night at the theater would be a disaster!

Name ____________________________________

Understanding a Play: "The Diary of Anne Frank"

Character	Personality Traits	Examples in Dialogue and Action
Anne		
Peter		
Mr. Frank		

Relationship	Description	Examples in Dialogue and Action
Anne and Mr. Frank		

Name ______________________________

Compare and Contrast

Two of the characters in these plays learn more about themselves. Complete the chart to compare and contrast their searches and what they find out.

	The Diary of Anne Frank	***A Better Mousetrap***
What challenges do Anne Frank and the Woman face?		
How do Anne and the Woman change?		

Name ______________________________

Critic's Corner

Think about one of the plays you have read in the *Focus on Plays* section. Think about the characters, the setting, the plot, and other details. Write a critical review of the play, telling what you liked and didn't like about it. Be specific. Use examples from the play to support your points.

Name ______________________________

Understanding a Play: "A Better Mousetrap"

Character	Personality Traits	Examples in Dialogue and Action
Man		
Woman		
Mouse		

What is funny about this play?

____

____

____

____

Name ______________________________

Confounding Compounds

Circle the ten words that are compound words in the dialogue below. Write each word in the first column. Then write the two smaller words that make up the compound words in the second and third columns. After you have written each compound word and its parts, use three of these compound words in a sentence of your own.

Solomon: You've left another mess in the hallway upstairs. We were supposed to split the chores fifty-fifty, but I'm doing all of the work by myself. I refuse to clean up after you.

John: Don't get so upset. I'll fix everything right after I finish eating my hot dog and reading the newspaper. I promise, by the end of the weekend, this house will look brand-new.

Compound Word	First Word Part	Second Word Part
____________	____________	____________
____________	____________	____________
____________	____________	____________
____________	____________	____________
____________	____________	____________
____________	____________	____________
____________	____________	____________
____________	____________	____________
____________	____________	____________
____________	____________	____________

____

____

Name ______________________________

Compound Words

A **compound word** is made up of two or more smaller words.

ship + yard = shipyard

To spell a compound word correctly, you must remember whether it is written as one word, as a hyphenated word, or as separate words.

Write each Spelling Word under the heading that tells how the compound word should be written.

One Word

____
____
____
____
____
____
____
____
____
____
____
____
____

With a Hyphen

____
____
____
____

Separate Words

____
____

Spelling Words

1. headache
2. warehouse
3. cupboard
4. old-fashioned
5. teammate
6. rattlesnake
7. blueberry
8. headquarters
9. space shuttle
10. baby-sit
11. handwriting
12. nighttime
13. self-respect
14. shipwreck
15. penknife
16. mother-in-law
17. wristwatch
18. handkerchief
19. bulletin board
20. software

Name ____________________

Spelling Spree

Clue Addition Add the clues to create a Spelling Word.

Example: group of workers + friend = teammate

1. not day + 3:00 p.m. = ____________
2. a color + a small fruit = ____________
3. where the hand meets the arm + small clock = ____________
4. large boat + terrible accident = ____________
5. infant + to rest in a chair = ____________
6. container for liquid + flat wooden plank = ____________
7. sits on top of your neck + pain = ____________
8. something to write with + something that cuts = ____________
9. can be a fist + printed or cursive = ____________
10. female parent + not out + a formal rule = ____________
11. not young + made or formed = ____________
12. houses your mind + place to live = ____________
13. announcement + plank = ____________
14. baby's toy + kind of reptile = ____________

Spelling Words

1. headache
2. warehouse
3. cupboard
4. old-fashioned
5. teammate
6. rattlesnake
7. blueberry
8. headquarters
9. space shuttle
10. baby-sit
11. handwriting
12. nighttime
13. self-respect
14. shipwreck
15. penknife
16. mother-in-law
17. wristwatch
18. handkerchief
19. bulletin board
20. software

Name ______________________________

Proofreading and Writing

Proofreading Circle the six misspelled Spelling Words in this critic's review of a play. Then write each word correctly.

Spelling Words

1. headache
2. warehouse
3. cupboard
4. old-fashioned
5. teammate
6. rattlesnake
7. blueberry
8. headquarters
9. space shuttle
10. baby-sit
11. handwriting
12. nighttime
13. self-respect
14. shipwreck
15. penknife
16. mother-in-law
17. wristwatch
18. handkerchief
19. bulletin board
20. software

***Space Hackers* a Bust**

I am sorry to report that attending the play *Space Hackers* will be a waste of your time. The plot is so bizarre that I am still recovering from the headache of trying to sort it all out.

The story takes place in an abandoned whearhouse in Silicon Valley. Cornelius Dingleberry, who plays the part of a brilliant soft ware developer, must work with his teamate to save a runaway space-shuttle. The dialogue is so poorly written that it would have been better for the actors to improvise their lines rather than to follow the script.

The only time that you will need a hankerchief at this flick is when you cry over the money you spent for the ticket. I hope veteran director Paul Blackadder directs another play soon to restore his self respect.

1. ______________ 4. ______________

2. ______________ 5. ______________

3. ______________ 6. ______________

Write a Review Suppose that you are another newspaper critic who liked the play *Space Hackers.*

On a separate sheet of paper, write a few paragraphs that give a positive review of *Space Hackers.* Use Spelling Words from the list.

Name ______________________________

Brand-Name Words

The diary entry below contains ten words that started out as trademarked brand names. As you read, circle each one you find.

Dear Diary,

I had a really great day today! I think it was all thanks to my new breakfast routine, which involves eating a big bowl of shredded wheat with hot sauce. That's right, hot sauce. It's my secret to waking up in the morning. Some people prefer coffee and cornflakes, but to each his own! After breakfast, I put on my Walkman, swept the linoleum, and rollerbladed off down the street to Teddy's house. When I got there, Teddy was taking aspirin and rubbing ice on his knee. He had a big rip in his Levi's and a bruise on his head. Teddy explained that he'd fallen while trying to skate backward down some stairs. His kneepads and helmet had fallen off because their velcro straps didn't stick. We rested for a minute and had a glass of Kool-Aid. Then I asked him if he felt well enough to go skating again, and he said yes. But when he suggested skating down an escalator, I gently talked him out of it.

Think of three other brand name words. Write a sentence for each new word.

____

____

____

____

____

____

____

Name ______________________________

Lion's Tale

Using Introductory Words Interjections, introductory words, and nouns in direct address can make dialogue in a play more realistic.

Write a word or a phrase from the box to begin each sentence, and follow it with the correct punctuation mark.

Lion	Oh no	Hurrah	Rabbit
Well	Hey	Grrr	Absolutely not

Rabbit is hopping through the forest. Suddenly a lion appears.

Lion: ______________ I'm going to eat you.

Rabbit: ______________ I'm glad I'll be eaten by a small, quiet beast instead of a big, loud one.

Lion: ______________ What are you talking about?

Rabbit leads Lion to a well, leaps onto the edge, and points down into it.

Rabbit: There's someone bigger and louder than you. Look!

Lion (*seeing his reflection*): ______________ Who do you think you are?

The lion's words echo from the well.

Lion: ______________ I'm the biggest, loudest beast in the forest!

The lion again hears his words echoed from the well.

Lion: ______________ I'll show you!

The furious lion bares his teeth and leaps into the well to attack his reflection. A splash is heard.

Lion: ______________

Rabbit: ______________ you may be the biggest, loudest beast in the forest, but I don't think you are the smartest one.

Name ______________________________

Of Mice and Cats

Points of Ellipsis Unfinished thoughts or pauses can help make play dialogue more realistic and lively. Use points of ellipsis, or three spaced dots, to show a pause or an unfinished thought.

Rewrite this dialogue. Make it more realistic and lively by adding five pauses or unfinished thoughts. Use points of ellipsis.

The mice are talking inside a mouse hole. Just outside, a cat is sleeping.

Mousely: That cat is giving me a headache!

Cheeser: Me, too. Every time I go out he sneaks up and tries to catch me. I can't go on this way!

Nibbles: You're right. We must do something.

Mousely: I have an idea. Let's put a bell on the cat so he can't sneak up on us.

Cheeser: That's a great plan. Do it now!

Mousely: Wait a minute! I'm a slow runner.

Nibbles: This was *your* idea.

____

____

____

____

____

____

____

____

____

Name ____

The Water Hole

Punctuating Play Dialogue Use an exclamation point with strong interjections. Use commas with introductory words, mild interjections, and nouns in direct address. Use points of ellipsis to show a pause or an incomplete thought.

Use proofreading marks to correct the twelve errors in punctuation in this play dialogue.

Proofreading Marks

- Indent
- Add
- Delete
- Capital letter
- Small letter
- Add Period
- Add Comma
- Add Quotes
- Transpose

Example: Wart Hog: Well, This looks like a nice water hole.

Wart Hog: Hey, you! This is my water hole.

Lion: Grrr I am the king, everyone makes way for me.

Wart Hog: No stay away! My tusks are the sharpest in the land.

Lion: Wart Hog I am going to chew you up, and then I'll

Wart Hog: Lion I am going to stomp you down, and then I'll . . .

Lion: Wait Do you see those vultures.

Wart Hog: Yes I see them.

Lion: They're waiting for one of us to die . . and one of us will, if we fight.

Wart Hog: Hmm maybe we should share this water hole.

Lion: Good idea!

Name ______________________________

Writing a Funny Play

Silly Character		
Appearance	**Habits, Gestures**	**Style of Speaking**

Other Characters	
Setting	

Plot	
Problem	**Solution**

Name ______________________________

Writing Stage Directions

This passage from a play has vague stage directions. Revise each numbered item so that an actor would clearly understand what to do.

Characters: Mom, Dad, Ed, Liz, Furhead the dog
Setting: the family car, on a long drive to Grandma's house

Ed: (1. *Looking somewhere*): I'm so bored, I can hardly breathe.
Mom: (2. *Seeing someone*): Why don't we all play a game? That will help pass the time! I love games! Guess which one is my favorite.
Liz: Please, Mom, not the license plate game. (3. *Liz makes an expression.*)
Dad: We used to play the license plate game when I traveled to visit my grandmother, with my parents. It must be a great family tradition! That will help us pass the next four hours, all right. (4. *Liz and Ed look at each other.*)
Furhead: Arf, arf! (5. *The dog moves.*)
Liz: Furhead! What are you doing? (6. *Liz does something to the dog.*)
Ed: See, Mom and Dad, even Furhead can't bear the license plate game. (7. *Ed speaks quietly to Furhead.*) Furhead, good dog, good dog.
Mom: Never mind about the game. I'll sing all my favorite Broadway show tunes to keep everyone from being bored! Which shall I sing first?
Dad: (8. *His voice changes.*): All of them, dear? Um, how about just one or two?

1. ______________________________
2. ______________________________
3. ______________________________
4. ______________________________
5. ______________________________
6. ______________________________
7. ______________________________
8. ______________________________

Name ______________________________

Growing Up

How do the characters in this theme grow? Add to this chart and the one on the next page after you read each story.

	Where the Red Fern Grows	Last Summer with Maizon
Who is the main character or characters?		
What problem does the main character have?		

Name ______________________________

Growing Up continued

	The Challenge	The View from Saturday
Who is the main character or characters?		
What problem does the main character have?		
What does the main character learn about himself or herself in the story?		

Sometimes struggle leads to growth. How do the stories in this theme support this statement?

____

____

Name ______________________________

Going to Market

Use the words in the box to complete the paragraph below.

Vocabulary

- provisions
- determination
- depot
- urgency
- wares
- cheap

Several times a year, people who live in the mountains load up their wagons and travel to town to sell homemade pies, jars of jam, and other ______________________________. It takes ______________________________ to rise before dawn and ride such a long distance. Restaurants in town are not ______________________________, so the mountain people usually bring their own food. They carry strips of dried meat and other ______________________________ in their packs. The travelers feel a sense of ______________________________ as they approach the town because they must hurry to set up their displays before shoppers from the city begin arriving at the train ______________________________.

Where the Red Fern Grows

Graphic Organizer
Generalization Chart

Name ______________________________

Generalization Chart

Generalizations	Information from the Story	Information from My Own Life
Page 247	Page 247	
Pages 248–252	Pages 248–252	
Pages 253–254	Pages 253–254	
Page 254	Page 254	
Pages 257–260	Pages 257–260	
Pages 262–264	Pages 262–264	

Name ______________________________

A Conversation with Papa

Suppose that Billy returns from Tahlequah, and must tell his parents where he's been and why. Below is a conversation he might have with his father. Use details from the story to help you fill in the words Billy might say.

Papa: Billy, where've you been? Your mother and I have been worried about you.

Billy: ______________________________

Papa: Why did you go there?

Billy: *(showing the bag with the hound pups)* ______________________________

Papa: Hound pups! Who'd you buy them from?

Billy: ______________________________

____

Papa: Those pups must be worth 30 dollars apiece! How'd you pay for them?

Billy: ______________________________

____

Papa: Where'd you get that much money?

Billy: ______________________________

____

____

Papa: Now wait a minute. How'd you order the puppies?

Billy: ______________________________

Papa: Why did you walk to Tahlequah by yourself? Did Grandpa tell you to?

Billy: ______________________________

____

Name ______________________________

Broadly Speaking . . .

Read the passage. Then complete the activity on page 199.

Dot and the Turkeys

All families were poor during the Great Depression. Dot's family was no exception. Even after selling milk and butter from the dairy farm, Ma and Pa struggled to keep food on the table for themselves and their seven children. The family's meals usually consisted of cornbread and buttermilk. Only on holidays did the children get treats such as nuts or a piece of fresh fruit. For children during the Depression, oranges were a particularly special treat. In general, families had little money for clothes, and often made their clothes by hand. Dot had no shoes and only owned one dress to wear to school, a homemade dress her older sister outgrew.

For a while Pa tried to make ends meet by raising turkeys. Ma had warned six-year-old Dot to stay away from the turkey pen. "Most turkeys are just plain mean," she said. Dot, however, was fascinated with the big birds and their drooping red wattles. She listened for hours to their clucking and gobbling and watched them strut about proudly. One day she slipped inside the pen to pet the huge, soft-looking birds. The turkeys, however, were not amused by the small girl inside their pen. The flock rushed at her and nearly smothered her. Dot's terrified screaming brought Ma and her brothers to her rescue. She never went near the turkeys again.

Where the Red Fern Grows

Comprehension Skill
Making Generalizations

Name ______________________________

Broadly Speaking . . . continued

Answer these questions about the passage on page 198.

1. The underlined sentence in the first paragraph states a generalization. Do you think it is valid or invalid? Why?

____

____

2. How could you rewrite this sentence so that it states a valid generalization?

____

3. What two generalizations about food are made in the first paragraph?

A. ______________________________

____

B. ______________________________

____

4. What two generalizations about clothes are made in the first paragraph?

A. ______________________________

B. ______________________________

5. How do the details about Dot's clothes support these generalizations?

____

6. What other generalization could you make about life during the Depression?

____

____

____

Name ______________________

Word Patterns in Writing

Add slashes between the syllables of each underlined word. Then write another sentence using the word correctly.

1. My hands were <u>calloused</u> after raking leaves all day.

____

2. The girl was <u>dumbfounded</u> by the sight of the vast prairie.

____

3. My sister and I like to tease our <u>grandfather</u> about his beard.

____

4. At the first light of dusk, the <u>mosquitoes</u> begin biting.

____

5. The boys saw a <u>shadowy</u> figure move in the window of the house.

____

Name ______________________________

VCV, VCCV, and VCCCV Patterns

To spell a two-syllable word, divide the word into syllables. Look for spelling patterns, and spell the word by syllables.

Divide a VCV word after the consonant if the first syllable has the short vowel pattern. Divide the word before the consonant if the first syllable ends with a vowel sound.

VC/V **bal / ance** V/CV **mi / nus**

VCCV words are usually divided between the consonants. They can be divided before or after two consonants that together spell one sound.

VC/CV **law / yer** V/CCV **au / thor** VCC/V **meth / od**

VCCCV words are often divided after the first of the three successive consonants.

When *y* spells a vowel sound, it is considered a vowel.

VC/CCV **sup / ply**

Spelling Words

1. balance
2. lawyer
3. sheriff
4. author
5. minus
6. method
7. item
8. require
9. supply
10. whisper
11. spirit
12. tennis
13. adopt
14. instant
15. poison
16. deserve
17. rescue
18. journey
19. relief
20. laundry

Write each Spelling Word under its syllable pattern.

VCV

____
____
____
____
____
____
____
____
____
____

VCCV

____
____
____
____
____
____
____

VCCCV

____
____
____

Name ______________________

Spelling Spree

The Third Word **Write the Spelling Word that belongs with each group of words.**

1. police chief, marshal, ______________
2. save, recover, ______________
3. demand, insist, ______________
4. editor, publisher, ______________
5. venom, toxin, ______________
6. earn, merit, ______________
7. liveliness, energy, ______________
8. ping pong, badminton, ______________
9. way, technique, ______________
10. object, article, ______________

Syllable Scramble **Rearrange the syllables in each item to write a Spelling Word. An extra syllable is in each item.**

11. jour di ney ______________
12. nus mi less ______________
13. yer pre law ______________
14. dol ance bal ______________
15. lief re ant ______________
16. a com dopt ______________
17. ex ply sup ______________
18. dry im laun ______________
19. per whis un ______________
20. in port stant ______________

Spelling Words

1. balance
2. lawyer
3. sheriff
4. author
5. minus
6. method
7. item
8. require
9. supply
10. whisper
11. spirit
12. tennis
13. adopt
14. instant
15. poison
16. deserve
17. rescue
18. journey
19. relief
20. laundry

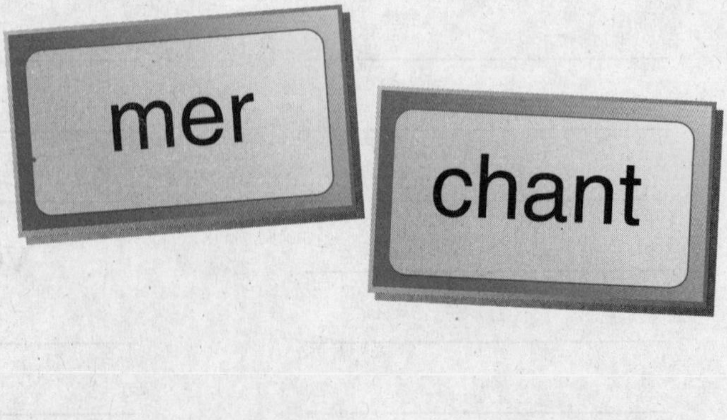

Name ________________________

Proofreading and Writing

Proofreading Circle the five misspelled Spelling Words in this advertisement. Then write each word correctly.

NEEDED: People needed to addopt one or more puppies. They are playful and full of spirrit, and they require lots of love and attention. They have been living in our londry room, but they still need to be housebroken. We will suply the first two weeks of food. These are great dogs, and they desserve a good home. Call 555-3647.

Spelling Words

1. balance
2. lawyer
3. sheriff
4. author
5. minus
6. method
7. item
8. require
9. supply
10. whisper
11. spirit
12. tennis
13. adopt
14. instant
15. poison
16. deserve
17. rescue
18. journey
19. relief
20. laundry

1. ____________
2. ____________
3. ____________
4. ____________
5. ____________

Write Guidelines for Pet Care Dogs, cats, and other pets need a great deal of care. What kinds of guidelines would a new pet owner need?

Choose a type of pet. Then, on a separate sheet of paper, write a list of guidelines for caring for that pet. Use Spelling Words from the list.

Name ______________________________

Synonym Sampler

Read each entry word, its definition, and its synonyms on the thesaurus page below. Then rewrite the numbered sentences using synonyms to replace the words in bold print.

happiness *n.* The state or quality of feeling joy or pleasure.

joy A feeling of great happiness or delight.
gladness The state or quality of feeling joy or pleasure.
bliss Extreme happiness; joy.

courage *n.* The quality of spirit that enables one to face danger or hardship; bravery.

spirit A mood marked by vigor, courage, or liveliness.
mettle Spirit; daring; courage.
bravery The quality or condition of showing courage.

1. Billy's **courage** helped him to reach his goal.

____

2. As he touched the pups, **happiness** welled up in Billy's heart.

____

3. Billy's **happiness** was hardly contained when he knew that the pups were about to come.

____

____

4. Billy needed extra **courage** to carry out his plan.

____

5. Billy's **courage** as he hiked through the hills was matched by his **happiness** when he arrived.

____

____

Name ____________________________

Summer Days

Verb Tenses The **tense** of a verb tells when the action takes place. The **present tense** is used when something is happening now, or happens regularly over time. The **past tense** is used when something has already happened. Here is how the verb *walk*, a regular verb, looks in these two tenses:

Present Tense	Past Tense
I **walk**.	I **walked**.
You **walk**.	You **walked**.
She/He/It **walks**.	She/He/ It **walked**.
We **walk**.	We **walked**.
You **walk**.	You **walked**.
They **walk**.	They **walked**.

Circle the verb in each of the following sentences. Decide whether the verb is in the past tense or the present tense, and write *past* or *present* on the line.

1. He lived in the Ozark Mountains. ____________
2. Celia fishes in the river. ____________
3. I strolled through the grass in my bare feet. ____________
4. They played with Kelly's new puppy. ____________
5. You like the outdoors. ____________

Now rewrite the five sentences above. If the original verb was in the past tense, change it to the present tense. If the original verb was in the present tense, change it to the past tense.

1. ____
2. ____
3. ____
4. ____
5. ____

Name ______________________________

Money!

More About Verb Tenses The **present tense** of a verb is used when something is happening now or happens regularly. The **past tense** of a verb is used when something has already happened. The **future tense** of a verb is used when something is going to happen. To form the future tense, use the helping verb *will* or *shall* with the main verb.

Circle the verb in each sentence. Then write its tense on the line.

1. We saved our allowance for a month. ______________
2. The package will arrive on time. ______________
3. William ordered new track shoes. ______________
4. We will earn money for our vacation. ______________
5. Pat saves for the future. ______________

Now rewrite each sentence using the verb tense shown.

1. **Future** ______________________________
2. **Present** ______________________________
3. **Present** ______________________________
4. **Past** ______________________________
5. **Future** ______________________________

Name ______________________________

When Did That Happen?

Choosing the Correct Verb Tense Switch tenses when you write only to tell about different times.

Dorinda wrote the following paragraph. Rewrite her paragraph using correct verb tenses. The first sentence will not change.

Every summer I visit my aunt and uncle. They lived in a mountain valley. I will like to walk there in my bare feet and waded in the creek behind their house. Last summer, I help my aunt and uncle with their vegetable garden. It is hard work, but we all will enjoy the vegetables. Vegetables fresh from a garden will taste so much better than vegetables from a store! Now I wanted to grow vegetables at home. When spring arrives, my parents helped me plant tomatoes and green beans. Then we enjoy eating vegetables from our garden.

____

____

____

____

____

____

____

____

____

____

____

Name ______________________________

Writing a Problem-Solution Composition

Writing about a character's problems in a **problem-solution composition** can help you better understand characters and events in a story. In *Where the Red Fern Grows*, for example, Billy Colman faces a problem. How Billy solves his problem reveals the kind of person he is.

Brainstorm problems that Billy solves in this story as well as problems that characters solve in other stories you have read. Write three of these problems and solutions on the graphic organizer below.

Problem		Solution(s)
Billy wants to buy two hound pups but does not have enough money.	→	He works hard for two years until he has saved fifty dollars.
	→	
	→	
	→	

Now pick one problem and its solution. On a separate sheet of paper, write your problem-solution composition. Begin with an introductory sentence that tells who or what you are writing about. Then state the problem in the first paragraph. In the second paragraph, describe how Billy or another character solves the problem. Include details that lead to the solution. Finally, end with a strong concluding sentence.

Name ________________________________

Organization

Good writers organize their ideas by sequence of events, by causes and effects, or by main ideas and details.

Help to unscramble this composition. Write students' ideas in a logical order in the organization outline below.

In the winter, he traps opossums and sells their hides to fur buyers.
Through hard work and determination, Billy finally realizes his dream.
Billy desperately wants to buy two hound pups.
Billy Colman is growing up during the Great Depression.
Also, he catches crawfish and minnows and sells them to fishermen.
To earn what he needs, Billy decides to work hard and save the money.
However, each dog costs twenty-five dollars.
During the summer, he picks berries and sells them.
After two years, Billy has saved fifty dollars.
Neither Billy nor his parents have fifty dollars to spend.

Paragraph 1: Introductory sentence

____

Problem

____

____

Paragraph 2: Solution

____

____

____

____

Concluding sentence

____

Name ______________________________

Revising Your Description

Reread your description. Put a checkmark in the box for each sentence that describes your paper. Use this page to help you revise.

Loud and Clear!

- ☐ My description is focused on single topic.
- ☐ Sensory words and vivid details create a clear picture.
- ☐ The details are told in a clear order. The beginning introduces the topic, and the ending sums it up.
- ☐ My writing shows my feelings about the topic.
- ☐ Sentences flow smoothly. There are almost no mistakes.

Sounding Stronger

- ☐ The description is not always focused on a single topic.
- ☐ More sensory words and vivid details are needed.
- ☐ The order could be easier to follow. The beginning and ending may be weak.
- ☐ Readers can't always tell how I feel about the topic.
- ☐ Many sentences are choppy. There are a few mistakes.

Turn Up the Volume

- ☐ There is no focus. It isn't clear what my topic is.
- ☐ There are no sensory words and almost no details.
- ☐ The order is unclear. There is no beginning and ending.
- ☐ My writing sounds flat. I show no feelings about my topic.
- ☐ Most sentences are choppy. There are lots of mistakes.

Reading-Writing Workshop

Improving Your Writing

Name ______________________________

Sentence Combining

Combine each pair of sentences to make them flow more easily. Use the joining word in parentheses. Add commas where needed.

1. Tom was born in Minnesota. (AND) Tom grew up there.

____

2. Toby was also born in Minnesota. (BUT) He grew up in Chicago.

____

3. Tom and Toby were twins. (AND) They had been separated at birth.

____

4. The twins had different last names. (BUT) They shared many traits.

____

5. Tom owned a beagle named Willie. (OR) Toby owned a beagle named Willie.

____

6. The other owned a cat named Billy. (OR) The other owned a cat name Millie.

____

7. Both twins loved baseball. (AND) Both twins hated fishing.

____

8. Both twins owned the same kind of truck.(BUT) Tom's was blue and Toby's was red.

____

____

9. They both liked the same movie. (OR) They both hated the same movie.

____

10. Once the twins were together, they were happy. (AND)
Once the twins were together, they would never part.

____

Name ______________________________

Words Often Confused

Do cows graze in a pastor or a pasture? Is a glass ring a bauble or a bubble? It is easy to confuse words that have similar spellings and pronunciations even though the meanings are different. The Spelling Words in each pair on the list are often confused. Pay careful attention to their pronunciations, spellings, and meanings.

Spelling Words

1. bland
2. blend
3. below
4. bellow
5. pastor
6. pasture
7. moral
8. mortal
9. bauble
10. bubble
11. bisect
12. dissect
13. assent
14. ascent

Write the missing letters in the Spelling Words below.

1. bl ____ nd
2. bl ____ nd
3. be ____ ____ ____
4. be ____ ____ ow
5. past ____ ____
6. pas ____ ____ ____ ____
7. mor ____ ____
8. mor ____ ____ ____
9. b ____ ____ ____ le
10. b ____ ____ ____ le
11. b ____ ____ ect
12. d ____ ____ ____ ect
13. a ____ ____ ent
14. a ____ ____ ent

Study List On a separate piece of paper, write each Spelling Word pair. Check your spelling against the words on the list.

Name ______________________________

Spelling Spree

Spelling Words

1. bland
2. blend
3. below
4. bellow
5. pastor
6. pasture
7. moral
8. mortal
9. bauble
10. bubble
11. bisect
12. dissect
13. assent
14. ascent

Contrast Clues **The second part of each clue contrasts with the first part. Write a Spelling Word to fit each clue.**

1. not a descent, but an _____ 1. ______________
2. not spicy, but _____ 2. ______________
3. not real jewelry, but a _____ 3. ______________
4. not a whisper, but a _____ 4. ______________
5. not living forever, but _____ 5. ______________
6. not a forest, but a _____ 6. ______________
7. not to cut into unequal pieces, but to _____ 7. ______________

Word Switch **For each item below, replace the underlined definition or synonym with a Spelling Word.**

8. Next week in my sister's biology class, they're going to cut apart in order to study frogs.
9. We were halfway up the mountain when we heard a cry for help from a lower position.
10. If you combine completely these red and yellow paints, you should get the right shade of orange.
11. Did your mom give her approval to our plan to go hiking?
12. The minister greeted the new couple the first time they walked into the church.
13. Each of Aesop's fables has a lesson.
14. There was a soap ball of air surrounded by a thin film of liquid on the surface of the dishwater.

8. ______________ 12. ______________

9. ______________ 13. ______________

10. ______________ 14. ______________

11. ______________

Name ______________________________

Proofreading and Writing

Proofreading **Circle the five misspelled Spelling Words in this movie description. Then write each word correctly.**

Spelling Words

1. bland
2. blend
3. below
4. bellow
5. pastor
6. pasture
7. moral
8. mortal
9. bauble
10. bubble
11. bisect
12. dissect
13. assent
14. ascent

Growing Up ★★★½ is a welcome change from the typical, blend children's movie. The director manages to bland four stories into one film. Together, they give a picture of the often difficult assent from childhood to the teenage years. Each story has its own morral, but teaches it quietly instead of trying to bellow it from the rooftops. Movie times are listed balow.

1. ______________
2. ______________
3. ______________
4. ______________
5. ______________

Two for One **Pick four word pairs from the Spelling Word list. Then, for each pair, write a sentence using both words.**

Name ______________________________

City Similars

Read the word in each box from *Last Summer with Maizon*. Then write a word from the list that is related to it in meaning. Use a dictionary if necessary.

Vocabulary

earlier
lifeless
porch
imagining
help
platform
communicate

express
____

desolate
____

daydreaming
____

previous
____

stoop
____

relieve
____

Name ______________________________

Inferences Chart

	Evidence from the Story	Own Experiences	Inference
How does Margaret feel about Maizon moving away? (page 279)			
How does Margaret feel about her friendship with Maizon once Maizon has left? (pages 280–281)			
How does Margaret feel about being in Ms. Peazle's class? (page 283)			
How do you think Margaret's classmates feel about her poem? (page 286)			

Name ____________________________

Story Frames

Think about what happened in *Last Summer with Maizon.* Write what happened in each part of the story by completing the story frames.

1. On the M train: Best Friends or Old Friends?

____
____
____
____

2. First Day in 6–1: The Essay

____
____
____
____

3. Next Day in 6–1: The Poem

____
____
____
____

4. On the Front Stoop: What's Changed? What Hasn't?

____
____
____
____

Name ________________________________

Reading Between the Lines

Read the passage. Then complete the activity on page 219.

The Audition

Serena ran into the girls' dressing room and locked the door behind her. "It's not fair! It's just not fair!" she cried, breaking into uncontrollable sobs. Just one week before, she had been on top of the world. She had been picked for the leading role in the spring musical. Mr. O'Toole, the choir director, had had the choir choose the parts by show of hands, after hearing the auditions for each part. "I won the part fair and square!" Serena wailed. "How dare Rebecca show up this week and ask to audition for my part! How could Mr. O'Toole have let her to do it? He's never done anything like that before! Rebecca should have been here last week if she wanted the part!"

The audition had been short, with only Serena and Rebecca performing. At first Serena hadn't been concerned. She'd won the part once, and she had figured that everyone would love her singing again. Mr. O'Toole had had everyone close their eyes again and raise their hands to vote. "The winner is Rebecca," Mr. O'Toole had announced. At that moment, the color had drained out of Serena's face as the choir applauded for Rebecca. Ashen-faced, she had bolted for the dressing room.

Name ______________________________

Reading Between the Lines

continued

Answer the following questions about the passage on page 218.

1. How does Serena feel when the choir votes for Rebecca?

2. What story clues help you figure out how she feels?

3. Why do you think Mr. O'Toole allows Rebecca to audition for the role even though the choir already picked Serena? (To answer, think about what is probably important to Mr. O'Toole as the choir director.)

4. How do you think Serena feels toward Rebecca at this moment in the story?

5. What do you know from real life that can help you figure out how Serena feels toward Rebecca?

Name ________________________________

Words, Inc.

For each word in column 1, write the base word in column 2 and the ending in column 3. Check a dictionary if you are unsure about the spelling of a base word.

	Base word	Ending
1. whispered	____________	____________
2. stumbled	____________	____________
3. exaggerated	____________	____________
4. sweating	____________	____________
5. smiling	____________	____________

Write the word from the chart that best completes each sentence.

6. When Margaret was unexpectedly asked to read her poem, she began ____________.
7. Her classmates ____________ among themselves.
8. They ____________ their reactions as she got ready to read.
9. Margaret ____________ over her feet on her way back to her desk.
10. When Margaret looked up, her teacher was ____________.

Name ______________________________

Words with *-ed* or *-ing*

Remember that when a one-syllable word ends with one vowel and one consonant, the final consonant is usually doubled before *-ed* or *-ing* is added. When a two-syllable word ends with a stressed syllable, double the final consonant before adding *-ed* or *-ing*.

map**ped** fit**ting** pilot**ing** begin**ning**

Write each Spelling Word under the heading that tells how the word is changed when *-ed* or *-ing* is added.

Spelling Words

1. mapped
2. piloting
3. permitting
4. beginning
5. bothered
6. limited
7. forgetting
8. reasoning
9. preferred
10. equaled
11. wondering
12. slipped
13. listening
14. fitting
15. pardoned
16. shoveled
17. favored
18. knitting
19. answered
20. modeling

8270 8270

Final Consonant Doubled

____

____

______________________ ______________________

______________________ ______________________

No Change

______________________ ______________________

______________________ ______________________

______________________ ______________________

______________________ ______________________

______________________ ______________________

______________________ ______________________

Last Summer with Maizon

Spelling Words with *-ed* or *-ing*

Name ______________________

Spelling Spree

Puzzle Play Write a Spelling Word to fit each clue.

1. posing for a photographer ◯ __ __ __ __ __ __ __ __
2. forgiven __ ◯ __ __ __ __ __ __
3. allowing __ __ ◯ __ __ __ __ __ __ __
4. flying a plane __ __ __ __ __ __ __ ◯
5. replied ◯ __ __ __ __ __ __ __
6. liked better __ ◯ __ __ __ __ __ __ __
7. was the same as __ __ __ __ __ __ ◯ __
8. making a sweater __ __ __ __ ◯ __ __ __ __ __

Now write the circled letters in order. They will spell the name of a character from *Last Summer with Maizon*.

__ __ __ __ __ __ __ __ __

Meaning Match Each item below contains a meaning for a base word followed by an ending. Add the base word to the underlined ending to write a Spelling Word.

Example: collect + ing = gathering

9. be suitable for + ing = ______________
10. be for or partial to + ed = ______________
11. the ability to think + ing = ______________
12. disturb or annoy + ed = ______________
13. fail to remember + ing = ______________
14. start + ing = ______________
15. plan in detail + ed = ______________

Spelling Words

1. mapped
2. piloting
3. permitting
4. beginning
5. bothered
6. limited
7. forgetting
8. reasoning
9. preferred
10. equaled
11. wondering
12. slipped
13. listening
14. fitting
15. pardoned
16. shoveled
17. favored
18. knitting
19. answered
20. modeling

Name ______________________________

Proofreading and Writing

Proofreading Circle the five misspelled Spelling Words in this letter. Then write each word correctly.

C

Dear Leslie,

How's it going? I've been lisening to the tape you sent with your last letter. It's great! I really like the song you sang at the beginning. I'm sorry it's taken me so long to write. My mom sliped on our sidewalk last week. She was shovelling snow. Since then, I've been doing a lot of things around the house. I guess my time is pretty limeted right now. Actually, I should get going. Mom must be wondring why the laundry hasn't been done. I 'll write again soon!

Your friend,
Carmen

1. ______________________
2. ______________________
3. ______________________
4. ______________________
5. ______________________

Spelling Words

1. mapped
2. piloting
3. permitting
4. beginning
5. bothered
6. limited
7. forgetting
8. reasoning
9. preferred
10. equaled
11. wondering
12. slipped
13. listening
14. fitting
15. pardoned
16. shoveled
17. favored
18. knitting
19. answered
20. modeling

Write a Poem Margaret wrote a poem to express her feelings about her father's death. Has there been an event in your life that caused you to feel great joy or sadness?

On a separate sheet of paper, write a poem about that event and the feelings you experienced then. Use Spelling Words from the list.

Name ________________________________

Finding Word Forms

Read each entry word, its inflected forms, and its definition. Write the form of the word that best completes each sentence.

choose (cho͞oz) *v.* **chose, chosen, choosing, chooses.** To decide.
close (klōs) *adj.* **closer, closest.** Near in space or time.
exchange (ĭks chānj′) *v.* **exchanged, exchanging, exchanges.** To give and receive mutually; interchange.
smart (smärt) *adj.* **smarter, smartest.** Intelligent, clever, or bright.
worry (wûr′ ē) *v.* **worried, worrying, worries.** To feel uneasy or concerned about something.

1. Maizon was the ________________ student at P.S. 102.
2. Margaret couldn't stop ________________ about whether Maizon would write to her.
3. Ms. Dell and Hattie ________________ cautious looks as they talked about Maizon.
4. Hattie felt that poetry ________________ where it wants to live.
5. Margaret moved ________________ to the women as they talked on the stoop.

Name ______________________________

Verb Trouble

Principal Parts of Regular and Irregular Verbs The **principal parts**, or basic forms, of a verb are the present form of the verb, the present participle, the past, and the past participle. All verb tenses are formed with these basic parts.

When the past and the past participle of a verb are formed by adding *-d* or *-ed*, the verb is **regular**. When the past and the past participle of a verb are formed in some other way, the verb is **irregular**.

	Present	Present Participle	Past	Past Participle
Regular	walk	(is) walking	walked	(has) walked
Irregular	ride	(is) riding	rode	(has) ridden

Margaret is having trouble with some verbs in a poem. The troublesome verbs are listed below. Complete the verb chart by writing the missing principal parts. Use a dictionary if needed. The first one is done for you.

Present	Present Participle	Past	Past Participle
sing	**(is) singing**	**sang**	**(has) sung**
write	(is)		(has)
search	(is)		(has)
feel	(is)		(has)
become	(is)		(has)
shout	(is)		(has)

Name ______________________________

Score with Perfect Tenses

- There are three **perfect tenses: present perfect, past perfect,** and **future perfect.** Form the present perfect tense with *have* or *has* and a past participle.
- Form the past perfect tense with *had* and a past participle.
- Form the future perfect tense with *will have* and a past participle.

Complete the chart below with the verb in the proper tense. The first one has been done for you.

Verb	Present Perfect	Past Perfect	Future Perfect
work	**have worked**	**had worked**	**will have worked**
move	have	had	will have
play	have	had	will have
write	have	had	will have
feel	have	had	will have
take	have	had	will have

Write the correct form of the verb in parentheses ( ) in each sentence below. Use the verb forms from the chart.

1. Maria ______________ (past perfect) away before school started. (move)
2. At the beginning of the year, my teacher ______________ (past perfect) with me after school. (work)
3. We ______________ (present perfect) together all day. (play)
4. I ______________ (present perfect) this way before. (feel)
5. In two weeks, she ______________ (future perfect) her report. (write)

Name ______________________________

Letter Perfect Tenses

Choosing the Correct Verb Form To correctly form a perfect tense, use the **past participle** form of the verb with *have*, *has*, and *had*.

Proofread the following letter that Margaret might have written to a friend who moved away. Insert the proper verb forms where needed.

Example: I had ~~took~~ taken the long route.

Hi!

It has been a long time since I have heared from you. Since you left, John K. has ask me about you six times! Sarita says, "Hi." Even Ms. Whitney has says she wonders how you are. J.D. has wrote you a letter, but he has not mailed it yet.

In the past month, I have went to the movies twice. Yesterday, I saw a TV movie called My Friend Flicka. I had seed it before but I still liked it.

Tomorrow I will have taked my fifth math quiz. We have one each week.

I plan to rake leaves and shovel snow to make money this year. By summertime, I will have save enough to visit you. Remember last summer when we goed to the beach? I had ran errands for months to earn that money.

Your friend,

Margaret

Name ______________________________

Responding to a Prompt

In *Last Summer with Maizon*, Ms. Peazle gives her sixth-grade class a writing prompt. She asks them to write an essay about their summer vacations. A **writing prompt** is a direction that asks for a written response of one or more paragraphs.

Read the following prompts and choose one you would like to respond to.

Prompt 1
Describe a time when you had to adjust to a change.

Prompt 2
Write about a person who is important to you. Describe the person and tell why he or she is important.

Prompt 3
Describe what you look for in a friend.

Use the chart below to help you plan your response. First, list key words in the prompt such as *compare, explain, describe,* or *discuss*. Next, jot down main ideas and details you might include. Finally, number your main ideas, beginning from most to least important.

Key Words	Main Ideas	Details

Write your response on a separate sheet of paper. Start by restating the prompt. Then write your main ideas and supporting details in order of importance from most to least important. Finally, check your response to make sure it answers the prompt.

Name ______________________________

Correcting Sentence Fragments and Run-on Sentences

Good writers check to make sure that their sentences are complete.

Rewrite the body of the letter on the lines below. Correct run-on sentences and sentence fragments so that the reader can understand them.

1234 Winding Drive Lane
Greenfield, Connecticut 06606
September 15

Dear Bethany,

How are you? Boarding school is okay I miss our old class. Teachers are pretty strict and they give tons of homework and they teach hard subjects. My tiny room at the end of the hall. Is already crammed with books and papers. Yesterday I met some other scholarship students. In my class. Unfortunately, none of them can jump rope.

I can't wait to come home on vacation Boston seems so far away. I miss you! Write soon.

Your friend,
Allison

____

____

____

____

____

____

____

____

Name ______________________________

What a Racquet!

Answer each of the following questions by writing a vocabulary word.

Vocabulary

- encourage
- notice
- conversation
- awkward
- managed
- bragged
- attention
- briskly

1. Which word tells what a show-off tries to attract?

____

2. Which word means "claimed to be great"?

____

3. Which word tells what friends do when they want you to do well? ______________________________

4. Which word describes how you might feel if you accidentally walked into the wrong classroom?

____

5. Which word means the same as *swiftly* and *rapidly*?

____

6. Which word could replace *was able* in the sentence "Willa finally was able to return a serve"?

____

7. Which word means "become aware of"?

____

8. Which word means "to have a discussion"?

____

Write two new questions of your own that use at least one vocabulary word each.

9. ____

10. ____

Name ______________________________

Story Map

Setting	Characters
______________________	______________________
______________________	______________________
______________________	
______________________	

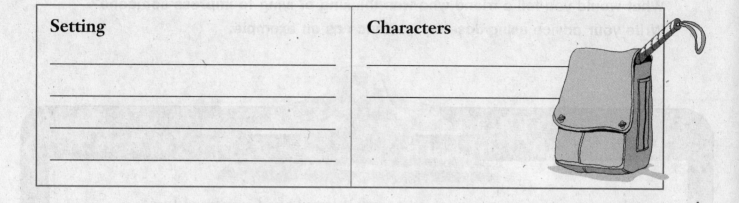

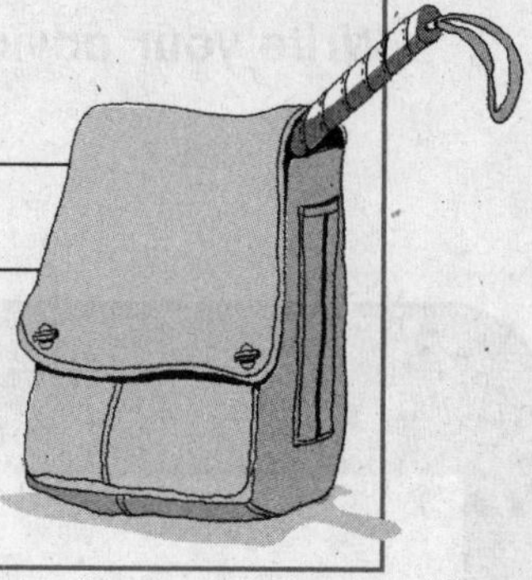

Plot

Story problem: ______________________________

____

Events:

1: ______________________________

____

2: ______________________________

____

3: ______________________________

____

4: ______________________________

____

Resolution: ______________________________

____

____

____

Name ______________________________

Give Advice

What would you tell a friend who was thinking of lying to impress someone? Write your advice using José's experience as an example.

Lying to impress someone won't work. I know of a boy named José who wanted to impress ______________________________.
He tried studying harder to ______________________________.
He even tried to show her ______________________________.
Nothing worked.

Then he saw that Estela had a ______________________________.
That gave him the idea to ______________________________.
Telling her that he could play racquetball was a lie, though, because ______________________________!

As soon as she said yes, José knew ______________________________.
He went to his uncle Freddy's house to ______________________________.
Uncle Freddy was sure ______________________________.

When José met Estela at the courts, he saw right away that ______________________________. Estela beat him ______________________________ Instead of impressing her, José just felt ______________________________.
So don't lie! Just be yourself.

Name ______________________________

Story Building Blocks

Read the story. Then complete the story map on page 234.

The Spelling Bee

Marty had been nervous all morning. The Lincoln Middle School Spelling Bee was about to begin, and he was the representative from Ms. Higgins's sixth-grade class. Ms. Higgins had asked Marty to compete earlier in the week. He'd said yes because he was a good speller and he thought it might be fun. However, now that he was up on the stage, he wondered what he could have been thinking. "What if I make a mistake and everyone laughs at me?" he worried.

The spelling bee began. Marty's first word was *nervous*. "What a perfect word for me," he thought. He spelled the word correctly, and his classmates applauded and cheered. Marty smiled gratefully. "This isn't so bad after all," he decided.

After three rounds, only Marty and an eighth-grade girl were left. Marty's next word was *enthusiastically*. "Wow. Long word!" he thought. He started spelling the word, and then stopped. He was trying to picture the word in his mind, but he couldn't remember the last letter he had spoken! Marty made a guess and continued at the *u*. When he finished, the judge said, "I'm sorry, Marty. The word has only one *u*." The spelling bee was over. Marty had lost.

As he was packing up his books, Marty saw Ms. Higgins. He was about to apologize when she said, "Marty, what a great job! You did better than all the seventh graders and most of the eighth graders!" Marty smiled. He hadn't thought about it that way. He hadn't lost. He'd finished near the top!

Name ______________________________

Story Building Blocks continued

Complete the story map with details from "The Spelling Bee."

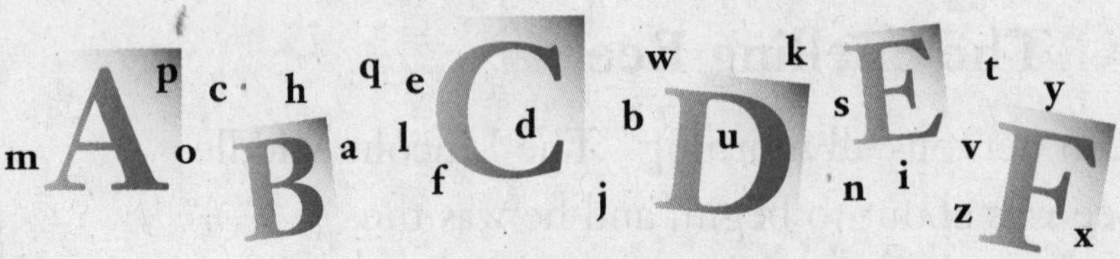

Story Map

Setting

When: ______________________________

____

Where: ______________________________

Characters

Who: ______________________________

____

Plot

Problem: ______________________________

Events:

1. ______________________________
2. ______________________________
3. ______________________________
4. ______________________________
5. ______________________________

____

Resolution: ______________________________

Name ________________________________

The Challenge

Structural Analysis Endings and Suffixes *-en, -ize,* and *-ify*

Suffix Chart

Read each sentence. For each underlined word, write the base and the suffix of the word in the chart. Then use sentence clues and what you know about the meaning of each suffix to write the meaning of each word. An example is provided.

1. José's class learned how the Egyptians would mummify their dead.
2. Estela's racket was blackened by her frequent playing.
3. She flattened her milk carton as she finished her lunch.
4. He tried to keep his face from reddening with shame.
5. José didn't want to dramatize his feelings, even though Estela could terrify him on the court.

Base word	Suffix	Meaning
mummy	-ify	make into a mummy

Name ______________________

Endings and Suffixes

Remember that if a word ends with *e*, the *e* is usually dropped when a suffix or an ending beginning with a vowel is added. The *e* is usually not dropped when a suffix beginning with a consonant is added.

divide + ed = divid**ed** grace + ful = grace**ful**

► In the starred words *mileage* and *manageable*, the final *e* of the base word is kept when a suffix beginning with a vowel is added.

Write each Spelling Word under the heading that tells what happens to its base word when a suffix or ending is added.

Final *e* Dropped

No Spelling Change

Spelling Words

1. graceful
2. divided
3. advanced
4. privately
5. replacement
6. excitement
7. adorable
8. heaving
9. forgiveness
10. mileage*
11. barely
12. forceful
13. scarcely
14. blaming
15. entirely
16. usable
17. sincerely
18. amusement
19. lifeless
20. manageable*

Name ______________________________

Spelling Spree

Adding Suffixes or Endings **Write the Spelling Word that has each base word below. The spelling of a base word may change.**

1. use ______________
2. forgive ______________
3. grace ______________
4. adore ______________
5. sincere ______________
6. heave ______________
7. mile ______________
8. life ______________
9. replace ______________
10. scarce ______________

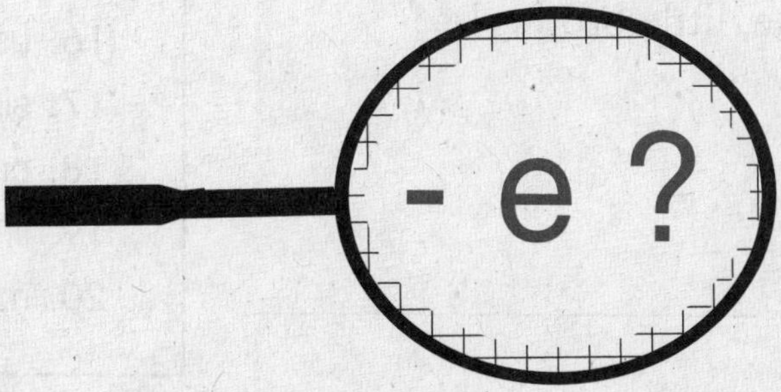

Spelling Words

1. graceful
2. divided
3. advanced
4. privately
5. replacement
6. excitement
7. adorable
8. heaving
9. forgiveness
10. mileage*
11. barely
12. forceful
13. scarcely
14. blaming
15. entirely
16. usable
17. sincerely
18. amusement
19. lifeless
20. manageable*

Contrast Clues **The second part of each clue contrasts with the first part. Write a Spelling Word to fit each clue.**

11. not united, but ______________
12. not partly, but ______________
13. not basic, but ______________
14. not publicly, but ______________
15. not impossible, but ______________

The Challenge

Spelling Endings and Suffixes

Name ______________________________

Proofreading and Writing

Proofreading Circle the five misspelled Spelling Words in this script for a scene from a movie. Then write each word correctly.

Setting: A basketball court, with a boy and girl playing.

LUCY: *(She makes a forcefull move to the basket and scores. Her face lights up with exitement.)* Yes!
DANIEL: *(His chest is heaving.)* That was a lucky lay-up. You barly got past me. If it wasn't for these old, worn-out shoes . . .
LUCY: *(She looks at Daniel with amusment.)* Quit blamming your shoes. It's my ball. The score's ten to ten. Next point wins.
DANIEL: Hold on! Let me catch my breath. . . . Okay, let's go.
LUCY: *(She gets the ball and shoots a graceful jump shot, which goes in.)* That's game, little brother!

Spelling Words

1. graceful
2. divided
3. advanced
4. privately
5. replacement
6. excitement
7. adorable
8. heaving
9. forgiveness
10. mileage*
11. barely
12. forceful
13. scarcely
14. blaming
15. entirely
16. usable
17. sincerely
18. amusement
19. lifeless
20. manageable*

1. ______________ 4. ______________

2. ______________ 5. ______________

3. ______________

Write a Challenging Invitation Are you especially good at a sport or game? Is there someone whom you'd like to challenge to be your competitor?

On a separate sheet of paper, write an invitation challenging a friend to compete against you in your chosen sport or game. Use Spelling Words from the list.

Name ______________________________

Using Parts of Speech

Read the dictionary entries. For each word, write two sentences, using the word as a different part of speech in each sentence.

► **palm** (päm) *n.* The inside surface of the hand. *–tr.v.* **palmed, palming, palms.** To conceal an object in the palm of the hand.

► **quiz** (kwĭz) *tr.v.* **quizzed, quizzing, quizzes.** To test the knowledge of by asking questions. *–n., pl.* **quizzes.** A short oral or written examination.

► **strain** (strān) *v.* **strained, straining, strains.** *–tr.* To exert or tax to the utmost. *–n.* An injury resulting from excessive effort or twisting.

► **whip** (wĭp) *v.* **whipped, whipping, whips.** *Informal.* To defeat; outdo. *–n.* A flexible rod or thong attached to a handle, used for driving animals.

1. ______________________________

____

2. ______________________________

____

3. ______________________________

____

4. ______________________________

____

Name ______________________________

The Irregular Verb Challenge

Irregular verbs have the past or past participle formed, not by adding *-ed* or *-d*, but in some other way. You must memorize the forms of irregular verbs. Here are five irregular verbs to study.

Present	Past	Past Participle
become	became	become
feel	felt	felt
go	went	gone
see	saw	seen
take	took	taken

Now cover the chart above, and complete the exercise below. Fill in the blank in each sentence with either the past or the past participle form of the verb in parentheses. Remember that there must be a helping verb in order to use the past participle form.

1. Bob had ____________________ a skilled tennis player. (become)
2. He ____________________ his racket to the court. (take)
3. He ____________________ confident. (feel)
4. Bob's friends had ____________________ him play many times. (see)
5. Last week they ____________________ to a big tournament with him. (go)

Name ______________________________

In Agreement

The verb in a sentence must agree in number with its subject. In the present tense, if the subject is singular, add *-s* or *-es* to the verb. Do not add *-s* or *-es* if the subject is *I* or *you* or if the subject is plural.

Kyle has started a conversation with Rosa, the new girl in his class. To find out what they are saying, choose from among these verbs to fill in the blanks. Make each verb agree with its subject.

smell	come	see
live	go	eat
taste	agree	
bake	take	

Kyle: This tomato soup ____________________ salty.

Rosa: You ____________________ from Ohio, don't you?

Kyle: Yes. My cousin still ____________________ in Ohio.

Rosa: My cousin does too! He ____________________ to college there.

Kyle: I ____________________ my cousin during the holidays.

Rosa: Our cafeteria chef ____________________ cookies every Friday.

Kyle: They ____________________ terrific!

Rosa: Chris and Kelly always ____________________ six cookies each.

Kyle: Our homework ____________________ a long time to do.

Rosa: I ____________________ with you!

Name ______________________________

Writing Challenge

Verbs That Agree The people below are facing challenges. Complete each sentence by writing an appropriate verb to describe each scene. Be sure that subjects and verbs agree.

1. Mark and Laura ______________________________.

2. A girl with three rings ______________________________.

3. Mary ______________________________.

4. Latasha and Bill ______________________________.

5. Roberto ______________________________.

The Challenge

Writing Skill Character Sketch

Name ______________________________

Writing a Character Sketch

A **character sketch** is a written profile that tells how either a real person or a character like Estela or José looks, acts, thinks, and feels.

Think about a real person or a story character from a selection you have read whom you would like to write about. Then use the web below to help you brainstorm details about this character's physical appearance and personality traits.

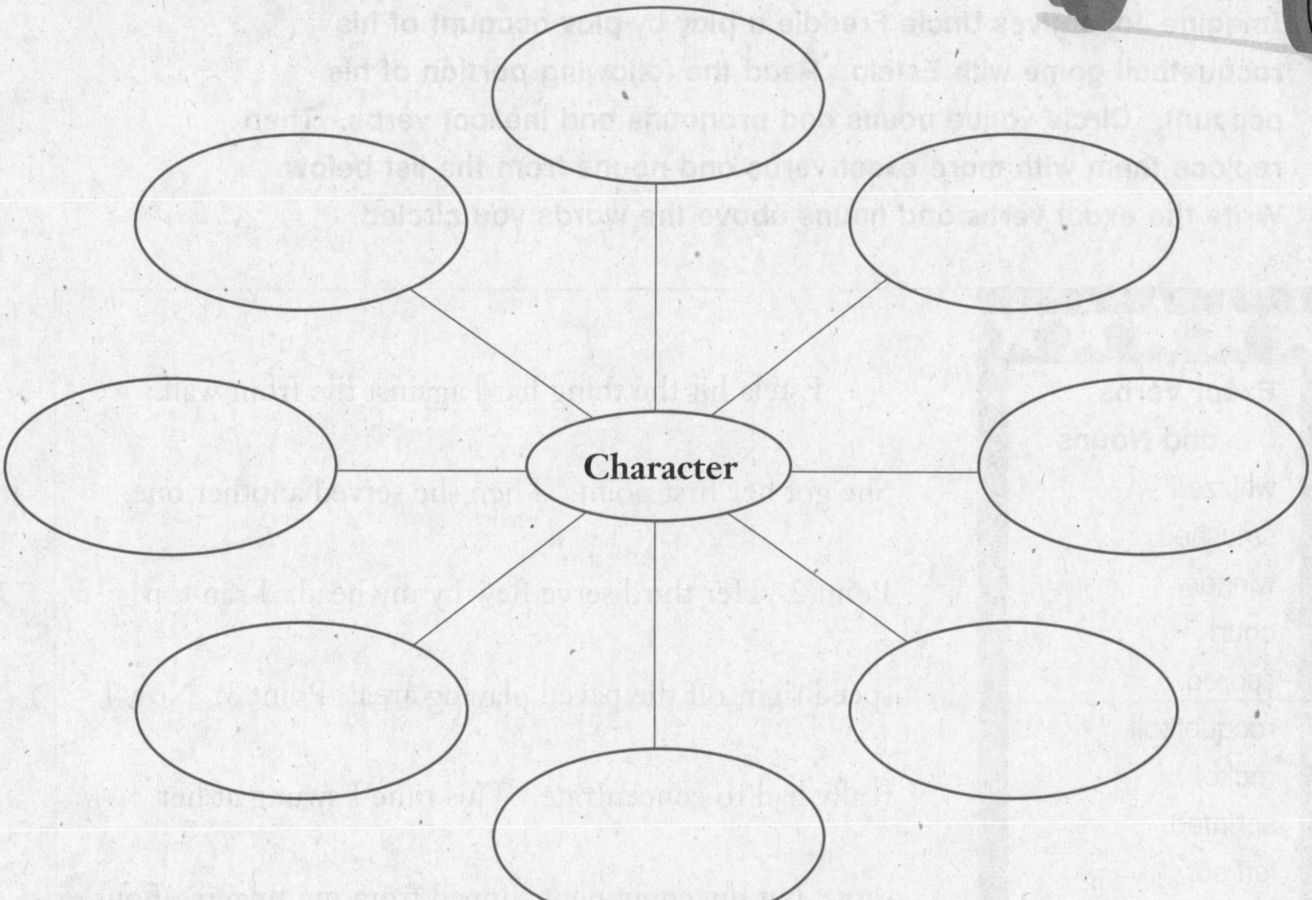

On a separate sheet of paper, write your character sketch. Begin with an anecdote or quote about the character. Then write a sentence that summarizes the character's most significant traits. Next, give two or three details from the web that support your summary. Conclude by restating the traits that are most significant.

Name ______________________________

Using Exact Nouns and Verbs

Which noun, *sport* or *racquetball*, is more exact? Which verb, *held* or *gripped*, is more exact? A good writer avoids using vague nouns and verbs. Exact nouns and verbs like *racquetball* and *gripped* will make your writing clearer and help readers get a more vivid mental picture of the people, places, and events you describe.

Imagine José gives Uncle Freddie a play-by-play account of his racquetball game with Estela. Read the following portion of his account. Circle vague nouns and pronouns and inexact verbs. Then replace them with more exact verbs and nouns from the list below. Write the exact verbs and nouns above the words you circled.

Exact Verbs and Nouns

- whizzed
- smashed
- winner
- court
- scored
- racquetball
- racket
- sprinted
- left ear
- swatted

Estela hit the thing hard against the front wall. She got her first point. Then she served another one. Point 2. Her third serve flew by my head. I ran top speed right off the paved playing area! Point 3. Now I really had to concentrate. This time I swung at her serve, but my equipment slipped from my fingers. Four to zip.

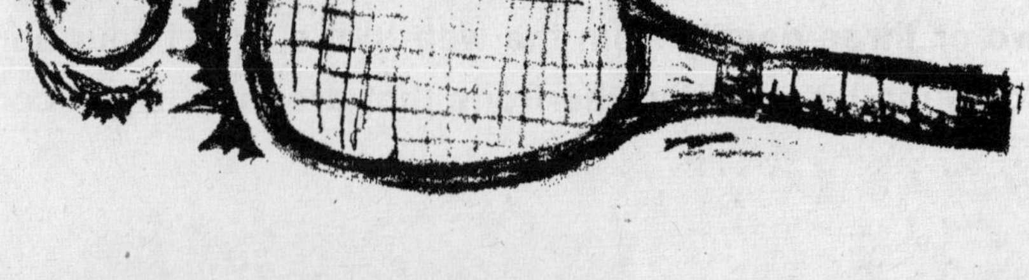

Name ______________________________

Turtle Patrol Puzzle

Words are missing in the sentences. Fill each blank with a vocabulary word. Then follow the directions to help you find the letters that need to be unscrambled to answer the question below.

Vocabulary

- subtle
- resettling
- volunteers
- interfering
- commute
- hover
- permitted

1. If you go back and forth between two places, you ____________________.

   Directions: Circle the fifth letter.

2. If you are moving to a new place, you are ____________________.

   Directions: Circle the first and seventh letters.

3. If something is not very obvious, it is ____________________.

   Directions: Circle the first and second letters.

4. If you remain in one place in the sky, you ____________________.

   Directions: Circle the third and fourth letters.

5. If something is allowed, it is ____________________.

   Directions: Circle the fifth and eighth letters.

6. If you and your friends offer to do something, you are ____________________.

   Directions: Circle the third and ninth letters.

7. If you are too curious about other people's business, you are ____________________.

   Directions: Circle the seventh letter.

8. What do turtle patrols try to do during big storms?

   h ◯ ◯ p t ◯ ◯ t ◯ ◯ ◯

   s ◯ ◯ v ◯ ◯ ◯

Name ______________________________

Problem-Solution Chart

Problem	Solution
If tall buildings hide the horizon's light, baby turtles head toward the city lights instead of the sea, and many die.	Turtle volunteers ______________
Nadia is jealous when she learns that Dad wants to be listed on Margaret's permit. She feels left out.	Nadia decides that, from now on, ______________
Dad knows that Nadia is upset and jealous of the time he spends with Margaret and the turtles.	Dad invites Nadia ______________
A storm hits the Florida Coast, and the turtles are in danger.	Nadia decides to ______________
Dad and Nadia realize that, like the turtles, they too need help settling into their new lives.	They agree that there will be times when they need a ______________

Name ______________________________

How Does Nadia Feel?

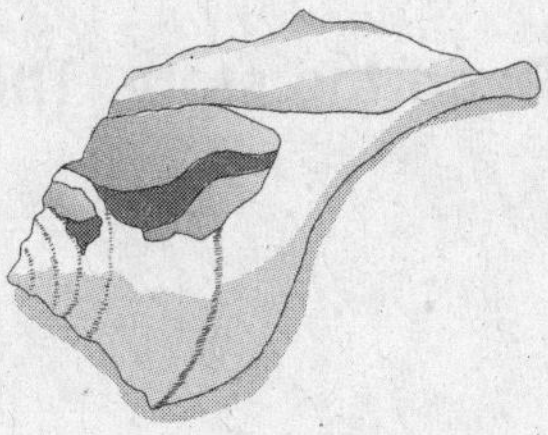

The following questions ask about how Nadia feels about her new family situation in *The View from Saturday.* Answer each one.

Why does it upset Nadia to learn that Margaret set up her mother's job interview?

____

____

____

Why does Nadia's father decide to take her to Disney World?

____

____

____

How does Nadia feel about her grandfather's remarriage and her new family at first?

____

____

____

Why does Nadia decide not to go to Disney World?

____

____

____

What connection does Nadia discover between her life and the lives of the sea turtles?

____

____

____

____

Name ______________________________

What Would You Do?

Read the story. Then complete page 249.

The Tag-Along

Ben whooped with joy as he rode down the hill on his mountain bike. He heard Ann shout with glee as she started down the same trail. When he glanced over his shoulder, however, Ben noticed that someone else was following them. It was Joyce. Ben felt annoyed.

Joyce had arrived in their class a few months ago. She was new to town and didn't know anyone. That became a problem for Ben when Joyce decided she wanted to become Ann's friend. For the past few weeks, no matter where Ben and Ann went, Joyce always seemed to show up a few minutes later.

Last week, Joyce came across Ben and Ann as they read comic books in Ben's tree house. She watched them for a while, but Ben did not invite her to join them. Yesterday, when Ann and Ben went swimming at the local pool, Joyce showed up and put her towel down right next to theirs.

Ben wanted to resolve the situation one way or another. He stopped his bike and waited for Joyce to catch up. He decided he was going to tell Joyce to stop following Ann around.

Name ______________________________

What Would You Do? continued

Complete the chart and answer the questions based on "The Tag-Along."

Character	Problem	Solution
Joyce		
Ben		

1. Is Joyce's way of dealing with her problem a good one? Why or why not?

____

____

____

2. How else can Joyce handle her problem?

____

____

____

3. Do you think Ben handles his problem in the best way possible? Explain your answer.

____

____

____

Name ______________________________

Prefix Puzzle

Each of the words in the eggs begins with the prefix *in-, im-, or con-*. Find the word that matches each clue and write it in the letter spaces.

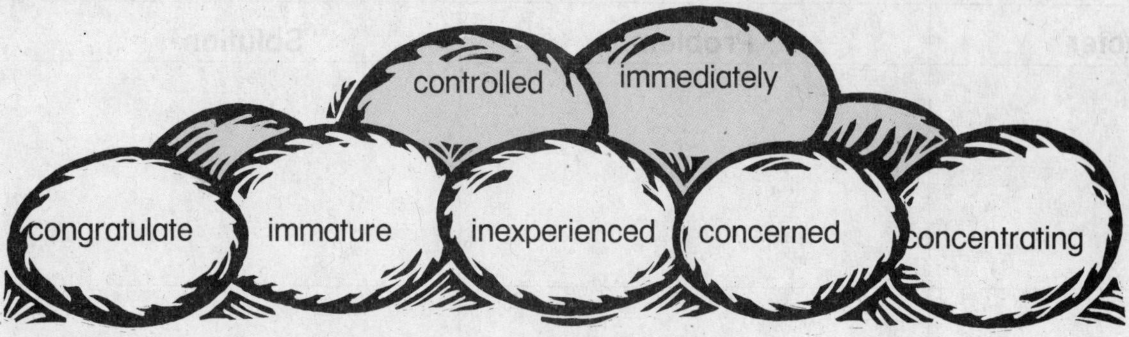

1. worried; anxious; troubled

2. held in check; restrained

3. not fully grown or developed

4. taking place at once; happening without delay

5. to express joy or good wishes to someone for an achievement

6. thinking very hard; focusing attention on something

7. not having knowledge or experience

Read the tinted letters down. Write the word, which means "to travel regularly between one place and another."

____

Name ____________________

Prefixes: *in-* and *con-*

A **prefix** is a word part added to the beginning of a base word or a word root to add meaning. A **word root** is a word part that has meaning but cannot stand alone.

The prefix *in-* is spelled *im* before a base word or a word root beginning with *m* or *p*. The prefix *con-* is often spelled *com* before the consonant *m* or *p*.

Prefix + Base Word	**Prefix + Word Root**
incomplete, **im**polite	**in**volve, **im**mense
contest	**con**trol, **com**ment, **com**pete

To spell words with these prefixes, find the prefix, the base word or word root, and any ending. Spell the word by parts.

Write each Spelling Word under the spelling of its prefix.

in-	*con-*
____________	____________
____________	____________
____________	
____________	____________
____________	____________
____________	____________

im-	*com-*
____________	____________
____________	____________
____________	____________
____________	____________
____________	____________

Spelling Words

1. computer
2. impolite
3. control
4. include
5. immigrant
6. compete
7. consumer
8. involve
9. immediate
10. comment
11. infection
12. concert
13. import
14. conversation
15. community
16. incomplete
17. immense
18. contest
19. inactive
20. complicate

Name ______________________________

Spelling Spree

Alphabetizing **Write the Spelling Word that fits alphabetically between the two words in each group.**

1. indoors, ______________________, inform
2. contract, ______________________, convene
3. compromise, ______________________, comrade
4. income, ______________________, increase
5. compass, ______________________, complain
6. inability, ______________________, incentive
7. consonant, ______________________, contain
8. concern, ______________________, conduct

Base Word/Word Root Match **Write the Spelling Word that has the same base word or word root as each word below.**

9. detest ______________________
10. export ______________________
11. exclude ______________________
12. duplicate ______________________
13. emigrant ______________________
14. politeness ______________________
15: immunity ______________________

Spelling Words

1. computer
2. impolite
3. control
4. include
5. immigrant
6. compete
7. consumer
8. involve
9. immediate
10. comment
11. infection
12. concert
13. import
14. conversation
15. community
16. incomplete
17. immense
18. contest
19. inactive
20. complicate

Name ______________________________

Proofreading and Writing

Proofreading Circle the five misspelled Spelling Words in these instructions. Then write each word correctly.

Instructions for Permitted Volunteers

1. Watch the hatching quietly. Keep conversasion to a minimum.
2. Don't involv yourself in the hatching process. Let the turtles do it!
3. The turtles' inmediate goal is to reach the water. Don't get in their way.
4. You will seem immence to the hatchlings. Don't stand too close to them.
5. Take notes about the results of the hatching. Include figures for all the eggs as well as for any dead or half-pipped turtles. Add a coment about anything unusual.

Spelling Words

1. computer
2. impolite
3. control
4. include
5. immigrant
6. compete
7. consumer
8. involve
9. immediate
10. comment
11. infection
12. concert
13. import
14. conversation
15. community
16. incomplete
17. immense
18. contest
19. inactive
20. complicate

1. ______________ 4. ______________

2. ______________ 5. ______________

3. ______________

Write a Personal Narrative Have you ever taken part in a project or program as a volunteer? What was the experience like?

On a separate piece of paper, write a personal narrative about a time when you served as a volunteer. Use Spelling Words from the list.

Name ______________________________

Connotation Correction

You are writing a screenplay for the selection, and the director would like to see some changes. Rewrite each sentence replacing the underlined word with a word from the box that has a negative connotation. Then rewrite it again using a word with a positive connotation. If you don't know the meanings of the words, use a dictionary to find them.

beamed	interrogated
chaperoned	invited
enthusiastic	smirked
fanatic	stalked

1. People who volunteer to help turtles can be excited about their work.

____

____

2. Nadia asked Ethan about the comments he had heard.

____

____

3. The volunteers followed the turtles as they moved from the beach to the sea.

____

____

4. Ethan smiled during the performance of *Phantom of the Opera*.

____

____

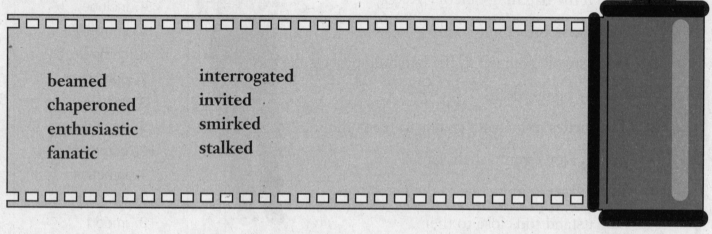

Name ______________________________

Up in the Sky

sit, set; lie, lay; rise, raise Some verb pairs can be confusing. Below are the definitions of three such pairs of words.

sit—to rest in an upright position
set—to put or place an object

lie—to rest or recline
lay—to put or place an object

rise—to get up or go up
raise—to move something up

Complete the sentences below by filling in the blanks with the correct verb in parentheses ( ) .

1. (sits/sets) A robin ____________ on its nest.
2. (lie/lay) I ____________ on my back to watch geese fly overhead.
3. (rises/raises) Mario ____________ from his chair when the flock flies over.
4. (sits/sets) That bird watcher ____________ down his binoculars.
5. (rise/raise) I ____________ at dawn when I go bird watching.
6. (lie/lay) I will ____________ my backpack on the grass.
7. (sit/set) We ____________ out food for the migrating birds.
8. (lies/lays) She ____________ under the tree listening to the chirping birds.
9. (sit/set) I ____________ the fallen baby bird back in its nest.
10. (rise/raise) I ____________ my binoculars to my eyes.

The View from Saturday

Grammar Skill *lend, borrow; let, leave; teach, learn*

Name ______________________________

Dog Days

lend, borrow; let, leave; teach, learn Here are the definitions of three more easily confused word pairs:

lend—to give
borrow—to take

let—to permit
leave—to go away

teach—to give instruction
learn—to receive instruction

Complete the sentences below by filling in the blanks with the correct verb in parentheses ( ).

1. Sadie ____________________ from Mr. Karol a book on dog training. (lends/borrows)
2. She ____________________ from the book how to train puppies. (teaches/learns)
3. Sadie and her puppy, Kipper, ____________________ for dog obedience school. (let/leave)
4. The instructor ____________________ Sadie how to handle her dog. (teaches/learns)
5. Sadie ____________________ me take Kipper to obedience school one day. (lets/leaves)
6. The instructor ____________________ me a better leash. (lends/borrows)
7. Kipper ____________________ to sit on command. (teaches/learns)
8. We ____________________ for home. (let/leave)
9. My parents ____________________ me have a puppy. (let/leave)
10. I ____________________ to be responsible for her well-being. (teach/learn)

Name ______________________________

Autumn in New England

Choosing the Correct Verb **Proofread the following passage written by a girl on her way to New England in the fall. Correct each incorrect verb form.**

Example: The libarian borrowed me a book. (lent)

Please leave me explain something. I like setting on Florida beaches, but when it is autumn, I'd rather head to New England. Teachers learn me better and I rise my hand more often when it is cool outside. I look forward to seeing the trees turn red and gold. I set in newly raked leaves and watch the sky. Sometimes my mother leaves me make hot chocolate with marshmallows, and I wonder who learns squirrels to gather nuts. When I come home, I sit my books on my desk and lie my good school clothes over a chair. By February I will want to lend a little warmth from Florida, and by June I will be ready to fly south again, but in autumn, I am a New England girl.

Name ______________________________

Writing a Speech

In *The View from Saturday*, Nadia gives an informal speech to persuade her father to let her help Grandpa with the sea turtles. Now you will write your own speech. Choose a topic listed below or come up with an idea of your own.

- Write a speech in which the mayor of the Florida town where Nadia lives thanks the turtle volunteers for their efforts.
- Write a speech to persuade local residents to clean up a beach or park.
- Write a speech to inform a group of children about what the turtle patrol's job is and why it is important.

Use the chart below to help you get started. First, identify the purpose of your speech—to entertain, to persuade, to inform, or to thank—and the audience to whom you will speak. Then jot down facts about the situation and reasons why you feel a certain way about it. Before you begin to write, number your ideas, in the order you in which you will present them.

Purpose	Audience	Facts and Reasons

Write your speech on a separate sheet of paper. At the beginning, mention whom you are addressing and the purpose of your speech. Then present your facts and reasons in a logical order. Finally, end with a conclusion that sums up or restates the purpose.

Name ______________________________

Audience

Speech writers not only keep in mind their purpose for writing but also the **audience** they are addressing. Their audience affects what they say and how they say it. When you write a speech, you need to use language and examples that will best reach your audience.

Read each of the following excerpts from different speeches. What audience do you think the speech writer most likely had in mind when writing the speech? Choose a possible audience from the list and write it on the lines.

Audiences
- family members
- voters
- environmental club members
- real-estate developers
- turtle patrol volunteers
- pet owners
- residents of Florida
- biologists
- young children
- fishing industry representatives

1. The Plum Beach condominium will offer lucky owners wonderful views from each unit, including a close look at this area's marine life.

   ____

2. Although small turtles used to be commonly available, stores no longer sell them. If you want to observe sea life at home and up close, you might consider buying tropical fish.

   ____

3. Thank you so much for a job well done! You greatly contributed to this year's successful turtle patrol. Most importantly, you have helped Florida's sea turtles.

   ____

4. Sea turtles face extinction. Some are hunted for their meat, and turtle eggs are sold as a delicacy. Tragically, beach-front development has also destroyed the traditional breeding grounds of some species.

   ____

Name ______________________________

Artwork Words

Write each word from the box next to its meaning.

Vocabulary

- apprentice
- nib
- consolation
- timidly
- highlights

in a nervous, careful way ______________

brightly drawn parts ______________

an assistant learning a trade ______________

an ink pen's point ______________

something that comforts ______________

Now use three words from the box in a short paragraph describing a scene at an art studio.

____

____

____

____

____

Name ____________________

Story Problems

Use the chart below to list problems the main characters of *The Ink-Keeper's Apprentice* and *Jerry Pickney* face and the solutions they devise to solve these problems. Look back at the stories if necessary.

	Problems	Solutions
The Ink-Keeper's Apprentice: Kiyoi		
Jerry Pickney		

Name ______________________________

Story Predictions

Use the chart below to make inferences about the main characters of *The Ink-Keeper's Apprentice* and *Last Summer with Maizon*. Look back at the stories if necessary.

	***The Ink-Keeper's Apprentice:* Kiyoi**	***Last Summer with Maizon:* Margaret**
Story Detail	______________ ______________ ______________ ______________	______________ ______________ ______________ ______________
What I Know	______________ ______________ ______________	______________ ______________ ______________
Inference	______________ ______________	______________ ______________

Name ______________________________

Inspirational Words

Choose the word from the Vocabulary box that best fits each definition below.

Vocabulary

- influence
- testimony
- springboard
- commitment
- climate

1. ______________________
something that helps launch ideas or activities

2. ______________________
an overall mood and spirit

3. ______________________
something that affects a person's life

4. ______________________
dedication to a cause

5. ______________________
a statement about what really happened

Name ______________________________

Test Practice

Use the three steps you've learned to write a personal response to both these questions about *Jerry Pinkney.* Make a chart on a separate piece of paper. Then write your response on the lines below. Use the checklist to revise your response.

1. What advice would you give someone who wants to become an artist? Use information from *Jerry Pinkney* and your own ideas.

____

____

____

____

____

____

____

____

____

____

____

____

Personal Response Checklist

- ✔ Did I restate the question at the beginning?
- ✔ Can I add more details from what I read to support my answer?
- ✔ Can I add more of my thoughts or experiences to support my answer?
- ✔ Do I need to delete details that do not help answer the question?
- ✔ Where can I add more exact words?
- ✔ Did I use clear handwriting? Did I make any mistakes?

Continue on page 266.

Name ______________________________

Test Practice continued

2. **Connecting/Comparing** Do you think it's important for adults to encourage children to develop their talents? Explain why you think as you do. Use your own experience, as well as details from both *Last Summer with Maizon* and *Jerry Pinkney*.

Personal Response Checklist

- ✔ Did I restate the question at the beginning?
- ✔ Can I add more details from what I read to support my answer?
- ✔ Can I add more of my thoughts or experiences to support my answer?
- ✔ Do I need to delete details that do not help answer the question?
- ✔ Where can I add more exact words?
- ✔ Did I use clear handwriting? Did I make any mistakes?

Read your answers to Questions 1 and 2 aloud to a partner. Then discuss the checklist. Make any changes that will improve your answers.

Monitoring Student Progress

Comprehension Skill
Making Inferences

Name ____________________

Inferring a Character's Feelings

Read the story. Then answer the questions.

The Wrestler

Clem paced back and forth behind the row of folding chairs where some of his teammates were sitting. Kelvin, the team's 95-pound wrestler, was in the middle of the wrestling mat on the other side. His match had just begun. Soon it would be Clem's turn.

Clem tried to relax, but he was finding it hard to breath. "Why did I join the wrestling team?" thought Clem. "Why do I always follow in my older brother's footsteps?" Clem shook his head. He wanted to remain focused.

Then, out of the corner of his eye, he saw Kelvin on his back, fighting not to get pinned. "Come on, Kelvin," thought Clem. "Get off your back." Kelvin somehow managed to squirm free and went on the attack. "Go, Kelvin, go!" shouted Clem. Seconds later, Kelvin had pinned his opponent.

Now it was Clem's turn. He took a deep breath, clenched his teeth, and ran to the center of the mat.

1. How does Clem feel about his upcoming wrestling match?

____

2. What story clues help you figure out his feelings?

____

3. Why do you think Clem joined the wrestling team?

____

4. What do you know from your own experience that helps you understand Clem?

____

____

Name ______________________________

Making the Right Choice

Read the story. Then answer the questions.

The Party Choice

Maya looked at the two birthday party invitations on the table. The one from Grace, her best friend, had arrived on Tuesday. Jessica's came just today. Both parties were scheduled for the same day at the same time.

Jessica was the new girl in class. She lived in the house on the hill with the swimming pool. Maya really wanted to go to that party to get a chance to swim in the pool and get to know Jessica better.

Maya looked at both invitations once more. She decided she would go to Jessica's party. "If I just pretend I didn't get Grace's invitation, I won't have to tell her I'm not coming," she thought.

1. What is Maya's problem?

____

2. How does she decide to solve her problem?

____

3. Do you think Maya's solution is a good one? Why or why not?

____

____

4. How else do you think Maya can handle her problem?

____

____

____

____

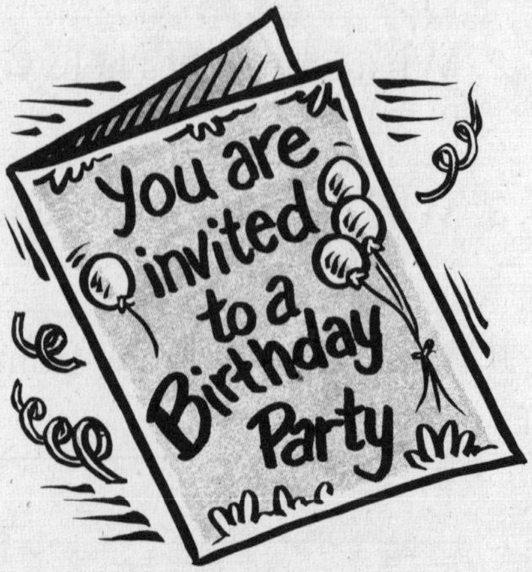

Monitoring Student Progress

Structural Analysis More Suffixes (*-en, -ize,* and *-ify*)

Name ______________________________

Meaning Matching

Read the base words in the box. Then read the sentences. Write the word from each sentence that contains one of the base words and the suffix *-en, -ify,* or *-ize.* Then write the meaning of the word.

glad	just	sign
harmony	sad	sympathy

1. The singer's voices harmonize beautifully.

____

2. The sounds of their voices gladden the audience.

____

3. I sympathize with the young boy who cannot see the stage.

____

4. When the lights come on, it will signify the end of the show.

____

5. The end of the show will sadden me.

____

6. Spending time at a concert is easy for me to justify.

____

Name ______________________________

Inflection Connection

Read each entry word and its definition. Pay attention to inflected endings such as *-s, -es, -ed, -ing, -er,* and *-est.* Then use inflected forms of each word to complete the sentences below.

cham•pi•on (chăm′ pē ən) *n, pl.* **cham•pi•ons**. Someone or something acknowledged as the best of all; have defeated others in competition.

com•pete (kəm **pēt′**) *v.* **com•pet•ed, com•pet•ing, com•petes.** To strive against another or others to win something; to take part in a contest.

de•liv•er (dĭ lĭv′ ər) *v.* **de•liv•ered, de•liv•er•ing, de•liv•ers.** **1.** To set free. **2.** To hand over. **3.** To give or utter.

edg•y (ĕj′ ē) *adj.* **edg•i•er, edg•i•est.** On edge; tense; nervous.

he•ro (hîr′ ō) *n, pl.* **he•roes.** A person noted for courage or special achievements.

hud•dle (hŭd′ l) *v.* **hud•deled, hud•dling, hud•dles.** To crowd together.

hard (härd) *adj.* **hard•er, hard•est. 1.** Resistant to pressure. **2.** Toughened. **3.** Requiring great effort; difficult.

vic•to•ry (vĭk′ tə rē) *n, pl.* **vic•tor•ies.** The act or fact of winning in a contest or struggle.

1. The students ____________________ together to decide who would be responsible for ____________________ the first answer.
2. If the team can win a series of ____________________, the members will be looked up to as ____________________.
3. Nadia seemed the ____________________ of all, knowing that it was the team's last chance to become the ____________________.
4. The teams were ____________________ fiercely.
5. Each event seemed ____________________ to win than the one before.

Name ____________________

Spelling Review

1–30. **Write each Spelling Word.**

1. ____________
2. ____________
3. ____________
4. ____________
5. ____________
6. ____________
7. ____________
8. ____________
9. ____________
10. ____________
11. ____________
12. ____________
13. ____________
14. ____________
15. ____________
16. ____________
17. ____________
18. ____________
19. ____________
20. ____________
21. ____________
22. ____________
23. ____________
24. ____________
25. ____________
26. ____________
27. ____________
28. ____________
29. ____________
30. ____________

Spelling Words

1. conversation
2. supply
3. minus
4. impolite
5. graceful
6. author
7. beginning
8. forgiveness
9. immediate
10. forgetting
11. slipped
12. method
13. answered
14. relief
15. consumer
16. heaving
17. amusement
18. include
19. advanced
20. listening
21. adorable
22. scarcely
23. excitement
24. control
25. balance
26. complicate
27. preferred
28. involve
29. community
30. lawyer

Name ____________________

Spelling Spree

Contrast Clues **The second part of each clue contrasts with the first part. Write a Spelling Word to fit each clue.**

1. not remembering, but ____________
2. not boredom, but ____________
3. not plus, but ____________
4. not simplify, but ____________
5. not asked, but ____________
6. not distress, but ____________
7. not retreated, but ____________

Code Breaker **Parts of some Spelling Words have been written in code. Use the code below to figure out each word. Then write the words correctly.**

@ = con	¤ = or	$ = ed	# = ing	* = ate
% = ance	+ = im	Ø = er	& = ation	¶ = ly

8. + medi * ____________
9. slipp $ ____________
10. bal % ____________
11. @ sum Ø ____________
12. heav # ____________
13. scarce ¶ ____________
14. @ vers & ____________
15. auth ¤ ____________

Spelling Words

1. relief
2. author
3. forgetting
4. consumer
5. slipped
6. conversation
7. minus
8. immediate
9. advanced
10. complicate
11. scarcely
12. heaving
13. answered
14. balance
15. excitement

Name ___________________________________

Proofreading and Writing

Proofreading Circle the five misspelled Spelling Words in these rules. Then write each word correctly.

Spelling Words

1. method
2. listening
3. lawyer
4. include
5. amusement
6. adorable
7. graceful
8. forgiveness
9. supply
10. control
11. impolite
12. preferred
13. beginning
14. community
15. involve

Rules for Growing Up

You can learn a lot by lissening to what older people say. Never be impalite to anyone. Keep your temper under controal. This might invollve biting your tongue once in a while, but it's worth doing. If you hurt someone's feelings, ask for forgivness.

1. ____________________
2. ____________________
3. ____________________
4. ____________________
5. ____________________

Write the Spelling Words that best complete this discussion.

Question: All of you must be 6. ____________________ to think about your futures. What kinds of jobs do you 7. ____________________ in your thinking?

Amy: I'd like to be a comedian! I love to see the 8. ____________________ on people's faces when I tell jokes.

Jaime: I'm 9. ____________________, so I might be a dancer. Later, if I 10. ____________________ to, I could teach dance.

Laura: As a vet, I'd have a steady 11. ____________________ of 12. ____________________ animals in my life!

Dion: I would like to be a 13. ____________________, like my mom. She helps people in the 14. ____________________ fight for their rights.

Bart: I'll invent a fast 15. ____________________ for growing up!

Write a Song **On a separate sheet of paper, write a song about growing up. Use Spelling Review Words.**

Name ______________________

Working with Verb Tenses

Underline the verb in each sentence. Then write the tense of the verb, *past, present,* or *future,* on the line.

1. Millie will learn from the elderly artist. ______
2. She sketched an elephant on her third day. ______
3. The artist picked her as his new apprentice. ______
4. The apprentices finish the cartoon panels for the master. ______
5. Millie will color the clothes in these cartoon panels. ______

Working in the order in which the sentences above appear, rewrite each sentence above using the indicated verb tense.

6. **Past** ______
7. **Future** ______
8. **Present** ______
9. **Past** ______
10. **Present** ______

Monitoring Student Progress

Grammar Skill Perfect Tenses

Name ______________________________

Writing Perfect Tense Verbs

Complete the chart below. Write the correct form of the verb in each column. The first one has been done for you.

Verb notice	Present Perfect have noticed	Past Perfect had noticed	Future Perfect will have noticed
1. use	have used	had used	will have used
2. attend			
3. take			
4. give			
5. become			

Write on the line below the correct form of the verb in parentheses after each sentence.

6. An artist ______________ the boy's talent last summer. (notice)
   past perfect
7. The boy ______________ oil paints and watercolo
   present perfect
8. By Friday the boy ______________ art school for three months. (attend)
   future perfect
9. He ______________ an excellent artist. (become)
   present perfect
10. His aunt ______________ him lessons before he started art school. (give)
   past perfect

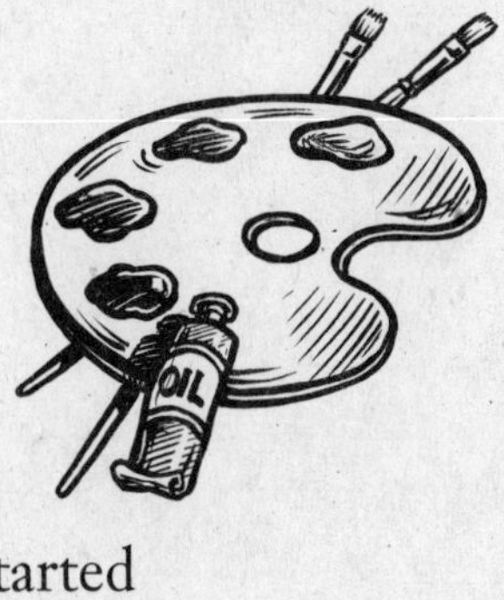

Student Handbook

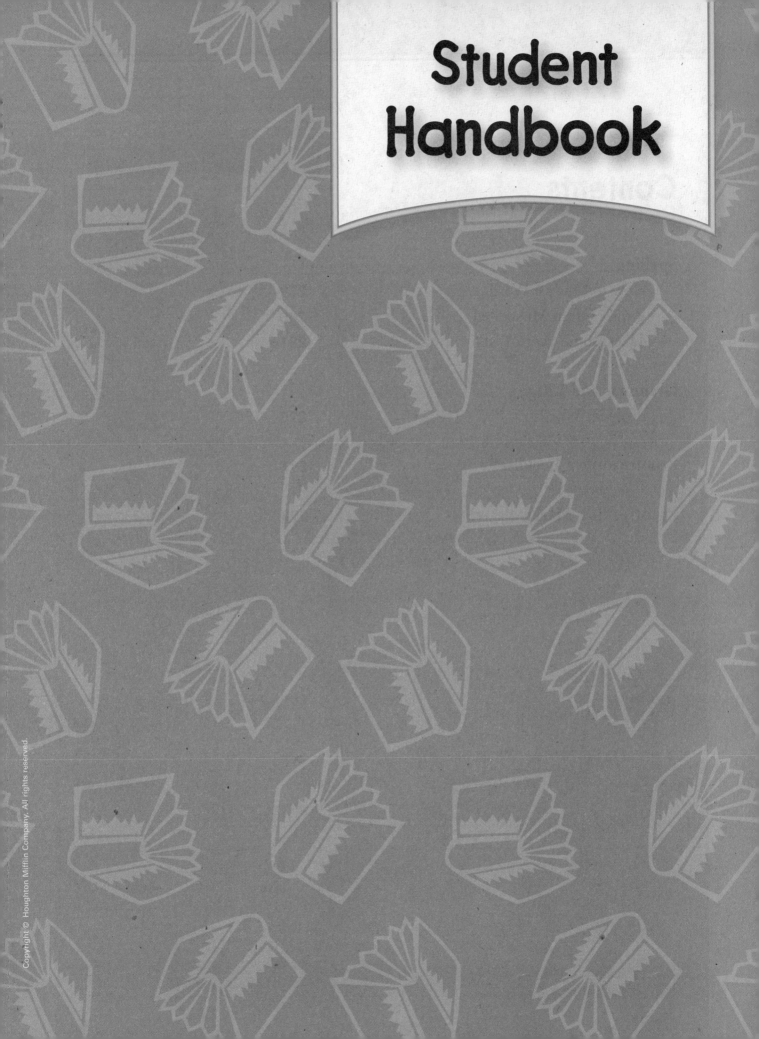

Contents

How to Study a Word

1. LOOK at the word.

- ► What does the word mean?
- ► What letters are in the word?
- ► Name and touch each letter.

2. SAY the word.

- ► Listen for the consonant sounds.
- ► Listen for the vowel sounds.

3. THINK about the word.

- ► How is each sound spelled?
- ► Close your eyes and picture the word.
- ► What familiar spelling patterns do you see?
- ► Did you see any prefixes, suffixes, or other word parts?

4. WRITE the word.

- ► Think about the sounds and the letters.
- ► Form the letters correctly.

5. CHECK the spelling.

- ► Did you spell the word the same way it is spelled in your word list?
- ► If you did not spell the word correctly, write the word again.

Words Often Misspelled

affectionate
again
all right
a lot
always
another
anyone
anything
anyway
applicable

beautiful
because
before
believe
brought
bureau

cannot
can't
captain
catastrophe
caught
clothes
coming
cousin

didn't
different
don't

eighth
embarrass
enough
essential
everybody
everything
everywhere

family
fatigue
favorite
field
finally
forfeit
friend

getting
going
guess
guy

happened
happily
haven't
heard
height
here

illustrator
indictment
instead
interpret
irreplaceable
its
it's

knew
know

might
millimeter
morning

o'clock
once

pennant
people
perceive
perspiration
pneumonia
pretty
probably

questionnaire

really
received
reversible
right

Saturday
school
someone
sometimes
stopped
stretch
sufficient
suppose
suppress
swimming

that's
their
there
there's
they're
thought
through
to
tonight
too
two

usually

weird
we're
whole
would
wouldn't
write
writing

your
you're

Words Often Confused

affect
effect

alley
ally

ascent
assent

bauble
bubble

bellow
below

bisect
dissect

bazaar
bizarre

bland
blend

confidant
confident

decent
descent

desert
dessert

eclipse
ellipse

hurdle
hurtle

illegible
ineligible

eminent
imminent

moral
mortal

pastor
pasture

sleek
slick

Take-Home Word List

Passage to Freedom

Long Vowels

/ā/	→	**gaze**, tr**ai**t
/ē/	→	th**eme**, pr**ea**ch, sl**ee**ve
/ī/	→	str**ive**
/ō/	→	qu**o**te, r**oa**m
/yo͞o/	→	m**u**te

Spelling Words

1. theme
2. quote
3. gaze
4. pace
5. preach
6. strive
7. trait
8. mute
9. sleeve
10. roam
11. strain
12. fade
13. league
14. soak
15. grease
16. throne
17. fume
18. file
19. toast
20. brake

Challenge Words

1. microphone
2. emphasize
3. refugee
4. pertain
5. coax

My Study List
Add your own spelling words on the back. →

Take-Home Word List

Courage
Reading-Writing Workshop

Look for familiar spelling patterns in these words to help you remember their spellings.

Spelling Words

1. your
2. you're
3. their
4. there
5. they're
6. its
7. it's
8. wouldn't
9. we're
10. to
11. too
12. that's
13. knew
14. know

Challenge Words

1. pennant
2. bureau
3. interpret
4. forfeit
5. perspiration

My Study List
Add your own spelling words on the back. →

Take-Home Word List

Hatchet

Short Vowels

/ă/	→	craft
/ĕ/	→	depth
/ĭ/	→	film
/ŏ/	→	bomb
/ŭ/	→	plunge

Spelling Words

1. depth
2. craft
3. plunge
4. wreck
5. sunk
6. film
7. wince
8. bomb
9. switch
10. length
11. prompt
12. pitch
13. else
14. cliff
15. pledge
16. scrub
17. brass
18. grill
19. stung
20. bulk

Challenge Words

1. habitat
2. cobweb
3. tepid
4. magnetic
5. deft

My Study List
Add your own spelling words on the back. →

Take-Home Word List

Name ____________

My Study List

1. ____________
2. ____________
3. ____________
4. ____________
5. ____________
6. ____________
7. ____________
8. ____________
9. ____________
10. ____________

Review Words

1. swift
2. tense
3. bunch
4. grasp
5. ditch

How to Study a Word

Look at the word.
Say the word.
Think about the word.
Write the word.
Check the spelling.

Take-Home Word List

Name ____________

My Study List

1. ____________
2. ____________
3. ____________
4. ____________
5. ____________
6. ____________
7. ____________
8. ____________
9. ____________
10. ____________

How to Study a Word

Look at the word.
Say the word.
Think about the word.
Write the word.
Check the spelling.

Take-Home Word List

Name ____________

My Study List

1. ____________
2. ____________
3. ____________
4. ____________
5. ____________
6. ____________
7. ____________
8. ____________
9. ____________
10. ____________

Review Words

1. greet
2. boast
3. brain
4. code
5. squeak

How to Study a Word

Look at the word.
Say the word.
Think about the word.
Write the word.
Check the spelling.

Take-Home Word List

Courage Spelling Review

Spelling Words

1. wince
2. league
3. strive
4. routine
5. prompt
6. strain
7. meant
8. foul
9. hoist
10. naughty
11. bulk
12. theme
13. mute
14. sponge
15. bloom
16. craft
17. throne
18. rhythm
19. vault
20. avoid
21. depth
22. roam
23. reply
24. stout
25. squawk
26. gaze
27. sleeve
28. ravine
29. sought
30. annoy

See the back for Challenge Words.

My Study List
Add your own spelling words on the back.

Take-Home Word List

The True Confessions of Charlotte Doyle

The /ou/, /o͞o/, /ô/, and /oi/ Sounds

/ou/ → **stout**
/o͞o/ → **bloom**
/ô/ → **vault, squawk, sought, naughty**
/oi/ → **avoid, annoy**

Spelling Words

1. bloom
2. stout
3. droop
4. crouch
5. annoy
6. vault
7. squawk
8. avoid
9. sought
10. naughty
11. mound
12. groove
13. foul
14. hoist
15. gloom
16. trout
17. noun
18. roost
19. clause
20. appoint

Challenge Words

1. bountiful
2. adjoin
3. nauseous
4. turquoise
5. heirloom

My Study List
Add your own spelling words on the back.

Take-Home Word List

Climb or Die

More Vowel Spellings

/ē/ → rout**ine**
/ĕ/ → sw**ea**t
/ī/ → c**y**cle
/ĭ/ → rh**y**thm
/ŭ/ → sh**o**v**e** (*o* consonant *e*)

Spelling Words

1. cycle
2. sweat
3. rhythm
4. rely
5. pleasant
6. routine
7. cleanse
8. shove
9. reply
10. meant
11. sponge
12. apply
13. threat
14. myth
15. deny
16. leather
17. rhyme
18. thread
19. meadow
20. ravine

Challenge Words

1. endeavor
2. oxygen
3. nylon
4. realm
5. trampoline

My Study List
Add your own spelling words on the back.

Take-Home Word List

Name ______________________

My Study List

1. ______________________
2. ______________________
3. ______________________
4. ______________________
5. ______________________
6. ______________________
7. ______________________
8. ______________________
9. ______________________
10. ______________________

Review Words

1. breath
2. measure
3. typical
4. deaf
5. crystal

How to Study a Word

Look at the word.
Say the word.
Think about the word.
Write the word.
Check the spelling.

Take-Home Word List

Name ______________________

My Study List

1. ______________________
2. ______________________
3. ______________________
4. ______________________
5. ______________________
6. ______________________
7. ______________________
8. ______________________
9. ______________________
10. ______________________

Review Words

1. scoop
2. moist
3. haul
4. loose
5. hawk

How to Study a Word

Look at the word.
Say the word.
Think about the word.
Write the word.
Check the spelling.

Take-Home Word List

Name ______________________

My Study List

1. ______________________
2. ______________________
3. ______________________
4. ______________________
5. ______________________
6. ______________________
7. ______________________
8. ______________________
9. ______________________
10. ______________________

Challenge Words

1. cobweb
2. tepid
3. refugee
4. coax
5. nylon
6. endeavor
7. oxygen
8. nauseous
9. bountiful
10. heirloom

How to Study a Word

Look at the word.
Say the word.
Think about the word.
Write the word.
Check the spelling.

Take-Home Word List

The Girl Who Married the Moon

Homophones
Homophones are words that sound alike but have different spellings and meanings.

Spelling Words

1. fir
2. fur
3. scent
4. sent
5. scene
6. seen
7. vain
8. vein
9. principal
10. principle
11. manor
12. manner
13. who's
14. whose
15. tacks
16. tax
17. hangar
18. hanger
19. died
20. dyed

Challenge Words

1. phase
2. faze
3. burrow
4. burro
5. borough

My Study List
Add your own spelling words on the back.

Take-Home Word List

What Really Happened? Reading-Writing Workshop

Look for familiar spelling patterns in these words to help you remember their spellings.

Spelling Words

1. tonight
2. everywhere
3. everybody
4. another
5. because
6. whole
7. people
8. cousin
9. clothes
10. height
11. always
12. right
13. might
14. really
15. everything

Challenge Words

1. essential
2. questionnaire
3. affectionate
4. illustrator
5. embarrass

My Study List
Add your own spelling words on the back.

Take-Home Word List

Amelia Earhart: First Lady of Flight

Vowel + /r/ Sounds
/ûr/ → skirt, urge, earth
/ôr/ → thorn, court
/är/ → chart
/îr/ → fierce

Spelling Words

1. fierce
2. sword
3. court
4. snarl
5. thorn
6. earth
7. skirt
8. chart
9. urge
10. yarn
11. whirl
12. mourn
13. rehearse
14. curb
15. earnest
16. starch
17. purse
18. birch
19. pierce
20. scorn

Challenge Words

1. circumstances
2. turmoil
3. absurd
4. territory
5. sparse

My Study List
Add your own spelling words on the back.

Take-Home Word List

Name ____________

My Study List

1. ____________
2. ____________
3. ____________
4. ____________
5. ____________
6. ____________
7. ____________
8. ____________
9. ____________
10. ____________

Review Words

1. pearl
2. stir
3. inform
4. pour
5. scar

How to Study a Word

Look at the word.
Say the word.
Think about the word.
Write the word.
Check the spelling.

Take-Home Word List

Name ____________

My Study List

1. ____________
2. ____________
3. ____________
4. ____________
5. ____________
6. ____________
7. ____________
8. ____________
9. ____________
10. ____________

How to Study a Word

Look at the word.
Say the word.
Think about the word.
Write the word.
Check the spelling.

Take-Home Word List

Name ____________

My Study List

1. ____________
2. ____________
3. ____________
4. ____________
5. ____________
6. ____________
7. ____________
8. ____________
9. ____________
10. ____________

Review Words

1. berry
2. bury
3. soar
4. sore

How to Study a Word

Look at the word.
Say the word.
Think about the word.
Write the word.
Check the spelling.

Take-Home Word List

Where the Red Fern Grows

VCV, VCCV, and VCCCV Patterns

VC|V:	**bal | ance**
V|CV:	**mi | nus**
VC|CV:	**law | yer**
V|CCV:	**au | thor**
VCC|V:	**meth | od**
VC|CCV:	**sup | ply**

Spelling Words

1. balance
2. lawyer
3. sheriff
4. author
5. minus
6. method
7. item
8. require
9. supply
10. whisper
11. spirit
12. tennis
13. adopt
14. instant
15. poison
16. deserve
17. rescue
18. journey
19. relief
20. laundry

Challenge Words

1. enhance
2. delete
3. precious
4. structure
5. decade

My Study List
Add your own spelling words on the back.

Take-Home Word List

What Really Happened? Spelling Review

Spelling Words

1. chart
2. starch
3. hangar
4. manner
5. gallon
6. whirl
7. curb
8. vein
9. similar
10. rural
11. sword
12. purse
13. hanger
14. manor
15. direction
16. mourn
17. who's
18. scent
19. channel
20. passenger
21. pierce
22. thorn
23. vain
24. struggle
25. frighten
26. rehearse
27. whose
28. sent
29. familiar
30. calendar

See the back for Challenge Words.

My Study List
Add your own spelling words on the back.

Take-Home Word List

Dinosaur Ghosts

Final /ər/, /ən/, and /əl/

/ər/ → messenger, director, similar
/ən/ → weapon, frighten
/əl/ → struggle, channel, mental

Spelling Words

1. struggle
2. director
3. weapon
4. similar
5. mental
6. frighten
7. channel
8. messenger
9. familiar
10. acre
11. error
12. gallon
13. rural
14. calendar
15. elevator
16. stumble
17. youngster
18. kitchen
19. passenger
20. quarrel

Challenge Words

1. agricultural
2. colonel
3. predator
4. corridor
5. maneuver

My Study List
Add your own spelling words on the back.

Take-Home Word List

Name ________________

My Study List

1. ________________
2. ________________
3. ________________
4. ________________
5. ________________
6. ________________
7. ________________
8. ________________
9. ________________
10. ________________

Review Words

1. matter
2. novel
3. mayor
4. consider
5. dozen

How to Study a Word

Look at the word.
Say the word.
Think about the word.
Write the word.
Check the spelling.

Take-Home Word List

Name ________________

My Study List

1. ________________
2. ________________
3. ________________
4. ________________
5. ________________
6. ________________
7. ________________
8. ________________
9. ________________
10. ________________

Challenge Words

1. territory
2. absurd
3. turmoil
4. phase
5. burrow
6. predator
7. colonel
8. faze
9. burro
10. corridor

How to Study a Word

Look at the word.
Say the word.
Think about the word.
Write the word.
Check the spelling.

Take-Home Word List

Name ________________

My Study List

1. ________________
2. ________________
3. ________________
4. ________________
5. ________________
6. ________________
7. ________________
8. ________________
9. ________________
10. ________________

Review Words

1. protect
2. effort
3. actor
4. credit
5. merchant

How to Study a Word

Look at the word.
Say the word.
Think about the word.
Write the word.
Check the spelling.

Take-Home Word List

The Challenge

Endings and Suffixes
divide + ed = divid**ed**
grace + ful = grace**ful**

Spelling Words

1. graceful
2. divided
3. advanced
4. privately
5. replacement
6. excitement
7. adorable
8. heaving
9. forgiveness
10. mileage
11. barely
12. forceful
13. scarcely
14. blaming
15. entirely
16. usable
17. sincerely
18. amusement
19. lifeless
20. manageable

Challenge Words

1. deflated
2. disciplined
3. consecutively
4. silhouetted
5. refinement

My Study List
Add your own spelling words on the back.

Take-Home Word List

Last Summer with Maizon

Words with *-ed* or *-ing*
map**ped** pilot**ing**
fit**ting** begin**ning**

Spelling Words

1. mapped
2. piloting
3. permitting
4. beginning
5. bothered
6. limited
7. forgetting
8. reasoning
9. preferred
10. equaled
11. wondering
12. slipped
13. listening
14. fitting
15. pardoned
16. shoveling
17. favored
18. knitting
19. answered
20. modeling

Challenge Words

1. propelling
2. equipped
3. transmitted
4. recurring
5. beckoned

My Study List
Add your own spelling words on the back.

289

Take-Home Word List

Growing Up Reading-Writing Workshop

Look for familiar spelling patterns in these words to help you remember their spellings.

Spelling Words

1. bland
2. blend
3. below
4. bellow
5. pastor
6. pasture
7. moral
8. mortal
9. bauble
10. bubble
11. bisect
12. dissect
13. assent
14. ascent

Challenge Words

1. imminent
2. eminent
3. illegible
4. ineligible

My Study List
Add your own spelling words on the back.

289

Take-Home Word List

Name ______________________

My Study List

1. ______________________
2. ______________________
3. ______________________
4. ______________________
5. ______________________
6. ______________________
7. ______________________
8. ______________________
9. ______________________
10. ______________________

How to Study a Word

Look at the word.
Say the word.
Think about the word.
Write the word.
Check the spelling.

Take-Home Word List

Name ______________________

My Study List

1. ______________________
2. ______________________
3. ______________________
4. ______________________
5. ______________________
6. ______________________
7. ______________________
8. ______________________
9. ______________________
10. ______________________

Review Words

1. ordered
2. planned
3. spotted
4. winning
5. gathering

How to Study a Word

Look at the word.
Say the word.
Think about the word.
Write the word.
Check the spelling.

Take-Home Word List

Name ______________________

My Study List

1. ______________________
2. ______________________
3. ______________________
4. ______________________
5. ______________________
6. ______________________
7. ______________________
8. ______________________
9. ______________________
10. ______________________

Review Words

1. breathless
2. collapsed
3. valuable
4. retirement
5. government

How to Study a Word

Look at the word.
Say the word.
Think about the word.
Write the word.
Check the spelling.

Take-Home Word List

Take-Home Word List

Growing Up
Spelling Review

Spelling Words

1. method
2. author
3. answered
4. forgiveness
5. complicate
6. supply
7. beginning
8. heaving
9. scarcely
10. include
11. relief
12. forgetting
13. amusement
14. excitement
15. consumer
16. balance
17. slipped
18. advanced
19. control
20. impolite
21. minus
22. listening
23. adorable
24. immediate
25. involve
26. lawyer
27. preferred
28. graceful
29. conversation
30. community

See the back for Challenge Words.

My Study List
Add your own spelling words on the back.

Take-Home Word List

The View from Saturday

Prefixes: *in-* and *con-*
in + active = **in**active
in + volve = **in**volve
in + polite = **im**polite
in + mense = **im**mense
con + trol = **con**trol
con + test = **con**test
con + ment = **com**ment
con + pete = **com**pete

Spelling Words

1. computer
2. impolite
3. control
4. include
5. immigrant
6. compete
7. consumer
8. involve
9. immediate
10. comment
11. infection
12. concert
13. import
14. conversation
15. community
16. incomplete
17. immense
18. contest
19. inactive
20. complicate

Challenge Words

1. imply
2. consequence
3. comprehensive
4. inadequate
5. communicate

My Study List
Add your own spelling words on the back.

Take-Home Word List

Name ____________________

My Study List

1. ____________________
2. ____________________
3. ____________________
4. ____________________
5. ____________________
6. ____________________
7. ____________________
8. ____________________
9. ____________________
10. ____________________

Review Words

1. concern
2. insist
3. compare
4. improve
5. convince

How to Study a Word

Look at the word.
Say the word.
Think about the word.
Write the word.
Check the spelling.

Take-Home Word List

Name ____________________

My Study List

1. ____________________
2. ____________________
3. ____________________
4. ____________________
5. ____________________
6. ____________________
7. ____________________
8. ____________________
9. ____________________
10. ____________________

Challenge Words

1. precious
2. enhance
3. beckoned
4. propelling
5. deflated
6. consecutively
7. refinement
8. communicate
9. imply
10. consequence

How to Study a Word

Look at the word.
Say the word.
Think about the word.
Write the word.
Check the spelling.

Take-Home Word List

Take-Home Word List

Take-Home Word List

Focus on Plays

Compound Words
A compond word is a word made up of two or more smaller words.

Spelling Words

1. headache
2. warehouse
3. cupboard
4. old-fashioned
5. teammate
6. rattlesnake
7. blueberry
8. headquarters
9. space shuttle
10. baby-sit
11. handwriting
12. nighttime
13. self-respect
14. shipwreck
15. penknife
16. mother-in-law
17. wristwatch
18. handkerchief
19. bulletin board
20. software

Challenge Words

1. windshield
2. guinea pig
3. self-conscious
4. videocassette
5. elementary school

My Study List
Add your own spelling words on the back.

Take-Home Word List

Focus on Poetry

Consonant Changes
A consonant that is silent in one word may be sounded in a word related in meaning.

Spelling Words

1. autumn
2. autumnal
3. muscle
4. muscular
5. crumb
6. crumble
7. sign
8. signal
9. bomb
10. bombard
11. haste
12. hasten
13. column
14. columnist
15. heir
16. inherit
17. hymn
18. hymnal
19. design
20. designate

Challenge Words

1. doubt
2. dubious
3. condemn
4. condemnation

My Study List
Add your own spelling words on the back.

Take-Home Word List

Name ______________

My Study List

1. ______________
2. ______________
3. ______________
4. ______________
5. ______________
6. ______________
7. ______________
8. ______________
9. ______________
10. ______________

Review Words

1. soft
2. soften
3. limb
4. limber

How to Study a Word

Look at the word.
Say the word.
Think about the word.
Write the word.
Check the spelling.

Take-Home Word List

Name ______________

My Study List

1. ______________
2. ______________
3. ______________
4. ______________
5. ______________
6. ______________
7. ______________
8. ______________
9. ______________
10. ______________

Review Words

1. salesperson
2. whoever
3. seat belt
4. highway
5. make-believe

How to Study a Word

Look at the word.
Say the word.
Think about the word.
Write the word.
Check the spelling.

Take-Home Word List

Problem Words

Words	Rules	Examples
bad	*Bad* is an adjective. It can be used after linking verbs like *look* and *feel*.	This was a bad day. I feel bad.
badly	*Badly* is an adverb.	I play badly.
borrow lend	*Borrow* means "to take." *Lend* means "to give."	You may borrow my pen. I will lend it to you for the day.
can	*Can* means "to be able to do something."	Nellie can read quickly.
may	*May* means "to be allowed or permitted."	May I borrow your book?
good well	*Good* is an adjective. *Well* is usually an adverb. It is an adjective only when it refers to health.	The weather looks good. She sings well. Do you feel well?
in into	*In* means "located within." *Into* means "movement from the outside to the inside."	Your lunch is in that bag. He jumped into the pool.
its it's	*Its* is a possessive pronoun. *It's* is a contraction of *it is*.	The dog wagged its tail. It's cold today.
let leave	*Let* means "to permit or allow." *Leave* means "to go away from" or "to let remain in place."	Please let me go swimming. I will leave soon. Leave it on my desk.
lie lay	*Lie* means "to rest or recline." *Lay* means "to put or place something."	The dog lies in its bed. Please lay the books there.

Problem Words continued

Words	Rules	Examples
sit set	*Sit* means "to rest in one place." *Set* means "to place or put."	Please sit in this chair. Set the vase on the table.
teach learn	*Teach* means "to give instruction." *Learn* means "to receive instruction."	He teaches us how to dance. I learned about history.
their there they're	*Their* is a possessive pronoun. *There* is an adverb. It may also begin a sentence. *They're* is a contraction of *they are.*	Their coats are on the bed. Is Carlos there? There is my book. They're going to the store.
two to too	*Two* is a number. *To* means "in the direction of." *Too* means "more than enough" and "also."	I bought two shirts. A squirrel ran to the tree. May we go too?
whose who's	*Whose* is a possessive pronoun. *Who's* is a contraction for *who is.*	Whose tickets are these? Who's that woman?
your you're	*Your* is a possessive pronoun. *You're* is a contraction for *you are.*	Are these your glasses? You're late again!

Proofreading Checklist

Read each question below. Then check your paper. Correct any mistakes you find. After you have corrected them, put a check mark in the box next to the question.

☐ 1. Did I spell all words correctly?

☐ 2. Did I indent each paragraph?

☐ 3. Does each sentence state a complete thought?

☐ 4. Are there any run-on sentences or fragments?

☐ 5. Did I begin each sentence with a capital letter?

☐ 6. Did I capitalize all proper nouns?

☐ 7. Did I end each sentence with the correct end mark?

☐ 8. Did I use commas, apostrophes, and quotation marks correctly?

Are there other problem areas you should watch for? Make your own proofreading checklist.

☐ ____________________

☐ ____________________

☐ ____________________

☐ ____________________

☐ ____________________

☐ ____________________

☐ ____________________

Proofreading Marks

Mark	Explanation	Examples
¶	Begin a new paragraph. Indent the paragraph.	¶The boat finally arrived. It was two hours late.
∧	Add letters, words, or sentences.	My ∧best friend ate lunch with me t∧oday.
	Take out words, sentences, and punctuation marks. Correct spelling.	We ~~looked at and~~ admired, the moddel airplanes.
≡	Change a small letter to a capital letter.	New York city is exciting.
/	Change a capital letter to a small letter.	The Fireflies blinked in the dark.
∨“ ∨”	Add quotation marks.	∨“Where do you want the piano?∨” asked the movers.
∧,	Add a comma.	Carlton∧, my cat∧, has a mind of his own.
⊙	Add a period.	Put a period at the end of the sentence⊙
∽	Reverse letters or words.	Raed carefully the instructions.
?	Add a question mark.	Should I put the mark here?
!	Add an exclamation mark.	Look out below!

My Notes

My Notes

My Notes

My Notes